Table of Contents

INTRODUCTION

No country in the world has more modern experience in stability operations than the United States. In fact, Afghanistan and Iraq were not the first countries this decade that the United States entered to liberate, rebuild, or stabilize. The United States liberated Kuwait in 1991, entered Somalia in 1992, Haiti in 1994, Bosnia in 1995, and Kosovo in 1999. Despite so much recent experience, the mission continues to be performed poorly with unlimited challenges.[1] Why? Regrettably, our national administration, consisting of the presidency, government agencies, and departments, failed to properly understand the types of conflict our nation was engaged in, failed to apply lessons from the past, and failed to properly resource the strategy to achieve our national interests. "If history repeats itself, and the unexpected always happens, how incapable must Man be of learning from experience?"[2] With respect to national security, the unexpected will happen and failure to learn should not be an option.

Framing the Problem

"The first, the supreme, the most far-reaching act of judgment that the statesman and commander have to make is to establish by that test the kind of war on which they are embarking; neither mistaking it for, nor trying to turn it into, something that is alien to its nature. This is the first of all strategic questions and the most comprehensive."[3]

---

[1] James Dobbins, *The Beginner's Guide to Nation-Building*, (Santa Monica: RAND Corporation, 2007), iii.

[2] George Bernard Shaw, *Man and Superman*, (Cambridge, MA: The University Press, 1903), 165.

[3] Carl von Clausewitz , *On War*, (New York: Knopf, 1993), 100.

Failing to understand the nature of conflict directly contributes to the failure of properly resourcing and implementing a balanced comprehensive strategy.

President Obama's analysis of our current wars succinctly, yet idealistically, concludes that our nation cannot exclusively count on military might alone.[4] To succeed along the entire spectrum of conflict, from peace to general war, the United States must fully understand the strategic environment, and within that environment, effectively integrate and balance all the instruments of national power. As General Omar Bradley reminds us, "Battles are won by the infantry, the armor, the artillery, and air teams, by soldiers living in the rains and huddling in the snow. But wars are won by the great strength of a nation—the soldier and the civilian working together."[5] This collaborative and coordinated approach, a blending of civilian and military power, is often referred to as a whole-of-government approach. Unfortunately, the U.S. government is unable to resource or implement this approach as desired by the President and our national leadership.

Recent experiences in combat have shaped the desire for resources that will be utilized to achieve U.S. strategy in the future, capable of spanning the entire spectrum of conflict, from stable peace to general war.[6] The integration of resources required, applied with the appropriate ways to meet national interests, is the whole-of-government approach to national security strategy.

---

[4] Barak Obama, "The Way Forward in Afghanistan and Pakistan," (Speech, Eisenhower Hall Theater, West Point, N.Y., December 1, 2009).

[5] United States Department of the Army, *Leadership Statements and Quotes: Department of the Army Pamphlet 600-65*, (Washington: U.S. Government Printing Office, 1985), 4.

[6] United States Department of the Army, *Operations:FM 3-0*, (Washington D.C., 2008), 2-1.

The whole-of-government approach is inaccurately considered a new idea or a new way to think differently about how the United States should address complex threats and problems presented in today's strategic environment. The current national security system was successful in defeating past conflicts in the Cold War era; however, with the challenges facing our nation today, there is a need for integrated planning and action across the full spectrum of conflict. "Currently, the system is not capable of effectively marshaling and integrating resources within and across federal agencies to meet such critical national security objectives."[7]

A whole-of-government approach reduces the reliance exclusively upon the military instrument of power by enabling federal agencies to integrate concepts that broaden the U.S. government's options and increases efficiency to solve national security challenges. By maximizing the contributions of all instruments of power, coordinated and collaborative, the whole-of-government approach communicates a unified effort between all government agencies.

Thesis

Despite an improved understanding of the strategic environment and a consensus that a whole-of-government approach must be employed to achieve our vital national interests, our nation falls short. *The DoD must be prepared to conduct a whole-of-government approach alone or with limited support from the other government agencies and departments; however, the DoD is currently unprepared, untrained, and under resourced to implement this approach effectively.* Secretary of State Hillary Clinton

---

[7] Project on National Security Reform, *Forging a New Shield*, (Arlington, VA: Center for the Study of the Presidency, November 2008), 13.

believes that "with a balance of civilian and military power, the United States can advance its interests and values, lead, and support other nations in solving global problems, and forge strong diplomatic and development partnerships with traditional allies and newly emerging powers."[8] Even with such eloquent rhetoric, the DoD routinely finds itself in control of all functions of government during stability operations with little or no assistance from non-DoD agencies and departments.

The U.S. government must realize that the civilian instruments of power currently have limited capability and capacity to contribute across the spectrum of conflict and throughout the entire continuum of operations. Unfortunately, understanding the requirement for a whole-of-government approach and likewise addressing it in a strategy document does not equal the ability to implement. With this realism, the DoD must be resourced and prepared to execute the whole-of-government approach independently or with little assistance, and, finally, civilian power must be incrementally improved—relieving the DoD from non-military responsibilities.

The DoD has failed to adequately address its own DoD Directive 3000.05, which directs the DoD to ensure that stability operations are given priority comparable to combat operations. In particular, it stresses that "U.S. military forces shall be prepared to perform all tasks necessary to establish or maintain order when civilians cannot do so."[9] Maintaining civil order in a protracted operational environment is far more intensive than martial law. It entails a host of skill sets and capabilities not resident in the military. The

---

[8] Hillary R. Clinton, "Leading Through Civilian Power," *Foreign Affairs*, (November/December 2010): 11.

[9] United States Department of Defense, Directive 3000.05, Military Support for Security, Stability, Transition and Reconstruction (SSTR), ([Washington D.C.]: Joint Chiefs of Staff, November 2005), 2.

reluctance of national leaders to properly address the *how* will continue to prevent our nation from effectively "maintaining or reestablishing a safe and secure environment, providing essential governmental services, emergency infrastructure reconstruction, and humanitarian relief in stability operations."[10]

"In recent years, many observers have concluded that the United States excels at winning wars, but has failed to develop interagency capabilities to win the peace."[11] This paper will explore the whole-of-government approach in order to define the most effective techniques and capabilities required to enable the DoD to conduct stability operations alone or with limited support from the other government agencies and departments. Additionally, the paper will offer a menu of options that allows the DoD to be the catalyst that drives and enables change within the national security system.

---

[10] United States Department of Defense, *Joint Operations: JP 3-0 Change 2*, ([Washington D.C.]: Joint Chiefs of Staff, 2010), GL-25.

[11] Brent Scowcroft and Samuel R. Berger, "In the Wake of War: Getting Serious About Nation-Building," *The National Interest*, no. 81 (Fall 2005): 49.

CHAPTER 1:
DEFINING THE WHOLE-OF-GOVERNMENT APPROACH

The whole-of-government "strategy is derived from a thorough assessment of the strategic environment and an appreciation of how to advance our national interests within it."[1] This blending of the instruments of national power across the full spectrum of conflict within the strategic environment is our nation's desired approach to achieving national interests. The strategy is not new, what would be new is if our nation actually resourced and then executed the strategy. To fully understand this whole-of-government approach as a strategy to achieve national interests, a baseline of understanding must be established. The instruments of national power, the current strategic environment, the continuum of operations, the full spectrum of conflict, and the current American war fighting paradigm will briefly be discussed. This chapter will establish the foundation and context for future analysis and study.

Instruments of National Power

Secretary of Defense Gates believes that "to meet the myriad of challenges around the world in the coming decades, this country must strengthen other important elements of national power, institutionally and financially, and create the capability to integrate and apply all of the elements of national power to problems and challenges abroad."[2] The instruments of national power need to operate as a system rather than a collection of separate components to maximize all available resources in a shared and balanced effort.

---

[1] United States, The National Military Strategy of the United States of America, (Washington, D.C.: White House, 2011), 21.

[2] The United States Department of Defense, "Civilian Expeditionary Workforce," http://www.cpms.osd mil/expeditionary/cew-secretary-message.aspx (accessed February 28, 2011).

The whole-of-government approach to achieving national interests is a concept that brings a unified effort between inter-governmental agencies to maximize all available resources in a collaborative effort.[3] What are these instruments of national power?

After an in-depth study of lessons learned from World War II, the National Security Act of 1947 (NSA-47) was created to organize and align the intelligence community, foreign policy, and the military. Loosely defined, these were considered the original instruments of national power. NSA-47 established several of the agencies that the President uses today to address national security issues. NSA-47 created the Department of the Air Force, renamed the Department of War to the Department of the Army, and included them with the Department of Navy in the new DoD. Further, the act created the National Security Council (NSC) and the Central Intelligence Agency (CIA). These organizations continue to be integral to applying the instruments of national power to manage and address today's national security issues.[4]

Similar to the analysis after WWII, the ability of the United States to achieve its national strategic objectives is dependent on the effectiveness of our government in not only employing instruments of national power, but effectively understanding them. "It is said that if you know your enemies and know yourself, you will not be imperiled in a hundred battles; if you do not know your enemies but do know yourself, you will win one and lose one; if you do not know your enemies nor yourself, you will be imperiled in

---

[3] Jason L. Percy and Terry A. Fellows Jr., "A Whole of Government Approach for National Strategy," (Master's Thesis, Naval Postgraduate School, 2009), 4.

[4] Stephen A. Cambone, *A New Structure for National Security Policy Planning*, (Washington D.C.: Center for Strategic and International Studies, 1998), 112-127.

every single battle."[5] One cannot balance, integrate, or employ what one does not understand.

Much has been discussed, argued, and debated about what actually makes up the instruments of national power, or the *whole*, in the whole-of-government approach. These instruments are defined in joint doctrine as diplomatic, informational, military, and economic— the tools the United States uses to apply power including its culture, human potential, industry, science and technology, academic institutions, geography, and national will.[6] President Obama ends the debate by specifically detailing in the NSS what instruments of national power must be integrated and balanced to achieve our national interests— defense, diplomacy, economic, development, homeland security, intelligence, strategic communications, the American people, and private sector.[7] Having defined the instruments of national power, the strategic environment in which they will be employed must be examined.

The Strategic Environment

The threats to national security are significantly different today than during WWII or even during the Cold War. The varied challenges to national security, ranging from terrorism to natural disasters, demonstrate that as the strategic environment evolves so must our system for national security.[8] The changing strategic environment should force a realignment and reorganization of

---

[5] Samuel B. Griffith and B. H. Liddell Hart, *The Art of War*, (New York: Oxford University Press, 1971), 101.

[6] United States Joint Chiefs of Staff, *JP 1-0: Doctrine for the Armed Forces of the United States* (Washington, D.C., 2009), I-8.

[7] United States, The National Security Strategy of the United States of America (Washington, D.C.: White House, 2010), 16.

[8] Ibid., 8.

today's national security system that will incorporate all government agencies and departments to create cooperation and collaboration in effectively dealing with the multitude of national threats.[9]

"Addressing new security challenges is less about an objective of dominance and more about predicting, preventing, and managing disruptions such as proliferation of weapons of mass destruction, terrorist acts, global contagions, and natural disasters."[10] This has led to the call for a whole-of-government approach to national security— an acknowledgment that "security comes from not only military strength, but also from the strength of diplomatic and humanitarian functions of government and non-governmental agents acting in a concerted fashion"[11]

Identifying the instruments of national power and understanding the strategic environment they will be employed in is fundamental to comprehending the whole-of-government strategy; however, understanding exactly when the approach will be utilized is often overlooked. Typically the whole-of-government approach is used in the context of stability operations; what is missing is the realization that the approach must be applied across the continuum of operations and within the full spectrum of conflict.

---

[9] Judith Evans, The Project on National Security Reform Releases Recommendations Urging Sweeping Changes to Improve the U.S. National Security System, (Washington D.C.: Project for National Security Reform, 2008).

[10] Kathy Gockel, "Meeting Complex Challenges Through National Security Reforms," *INSS Proceedings* (October 2008): 6.

[11] D.A. Brook and P.J. Candreva, "Whither the Defense Budget?," *Journal of Financial Management* (Spring, 2008): 14.

Continuum of Operations

Understanding the strategic environment leads one to understand that today and in the future, U.S. military forces will be engaged in a combination of combat, security engagement, and relief and reconstruction.[12] Joint Publication (JP) 3-0 defines this range of operations as the continuum of operations , military operations varying in size, purpose, and combat intensity within a range that extends from military engagement, security cooperation, and deterrence activities to crisis response and limited contingency operations and, if necessary, major operations and campaigns.[13]

"In today's strategic environment, the presence, reach, and capability of U.S. military forces, working with like-minded partners, will continue to be called upon to protect our national interests."[14] Like minded partners *are* the other instruments of national power. "The strategic environment requires the whole-of-government to engage in several types of operations simultaneously across the range of military operations. Commanders must combine and sequence offensive, defensive, and stability operations and activities to achieve the objective." [15] A particular type of operation is not doctrinally fixed and could shift within that range, for example, counterinsurgency operations that escalate from a security cooperation activity into a major operation or campaign.[16] Clearly a lot has been studied and written about the military instrument of power across the continuum of operations, although not explicitly stated, the role of the

---

[12] Joint Operations, II-24.

[13] Ibid., I-7.

[14] United States Joint Forces Command, *The Joint Operating Environment (*Norfolk, VA*.,* 2008), 4.

[15] Joint Operations, I-8.

[16] Ibid., I-8.

other instruments are as equally important across this continuum and the full spectrum of conflict.

The Full Spectrum of Conflict

The whole-of-government, civilian and military power, will be employed in offensive, defensive, and stability operations simultaneously within a range of conflict, from peace to general war. As the Department of State (DoS) has already realized, "the capability to provide stabilization and reconstruction must not be relegated only to post-conflict situations. Indeed, the nature of the world and the tasks ahead may dictate that the United States and its allies prevent rather than preempt whenever possible."[17] Prevent, preempt, and post-conflict have a time and space relationship with respect to violence, this relationship is referred to as the full spectrum of conflict.

> The full spectrum of conflict places levels of violence on an ascending scale marked by graduated steps. The spectrum of conflict spans from stable peace to general war including intermediate levels of unstable peace and insurgency. In practice, violent conflict does not proceed smoothly from unstable peace through insurgency to general war and back again.[18]

Levels of violence will jump from one point on the spectrum to another. General war may end in an unstable peace or unstable peace could erupt into general war.[19] Iraq is a recent example where general war ignited additional violence producing an insurgency, creating greater regional instability which threatens our national interests. Stable peace, unstable peace, insurgency, and general war are not a limited set; rather a tool to understand and visualize the levels of violence and the corresponding role of

---

[17] Hans Binnedijk and Stuart E. Johnson, *Transforming for Stability Operations*, (National Defense University, Center for Technology and National Security Policy, 2004), xv.

[18] *Operations*, II-12.

[19] Ibid., II-13.

instruments of national power in resolving conflict.[20] For the whole-of-government

approach to balance and integrate the instruments of power in the continuum of

operations, understanding where along the spectrum of conflict our effort resides helps to

improve how the instruments will be used.

Current War Fighting Paradigm

A framework for implementation of the whole-of-government approach is

established by fully understanding the strategic environment and *how* the instruments of

power will be employed across the full spectrum of conflict. However, limits to the use

of specific instruments, in particular the military, will dictate the employment of others.

If the instrument of military power cannot be utilized optimally, then this directly affects

the implementation of the other instruments. Exploring the two most recent large-scale

conflicts, Afghanistan and Iraq, a generalization as to the implementation of military

force as an instrument of national power can be deduced. This generalization is the

current American war fighting paradigm.

The paradigm is critical in understanding the most essential aspect of the strategic

environment that will exist along the spectrum of conflict— will the environment be

permissive or non-permissive for civilians? Civilian personnel are not well-suited to

operate in a combat environment, and U.S. departments and agencies generally do not

have extra personnel and funding that they can use to surge for military operations.

Therefore, if the strategic environment is not permissive, then the whole-of-government

approach cannot be implemented as understood by the national administration. Recent

experiences in Afghanistan and Iraq establishes the current paradigm.

---

[20] Operations, II-1.

12

After the refusal of the Taliban regime to cease harboring al-Qaeda, on October 7, 2001, the U.S. government launched military operations in Afghanistan. Operations were conducted with a force comprised of CIA operatives, an Afghanistan tribal alliance, air delivered precision munitions, and a very limited number of special operation soldiers from the 5th Special Forces Group on the ground.[21] On December 7, 2001, the Taliban surrendered their last stronghold, Kandahar, leaving Afghanistan in control of the Northern Alliance supported by U.S. forces and Pashtun allies.[22] An initial success that would evolve into today's continuing insurgency.

In September 2009, a report circulated that a classified assessment of the war in Afghanistan by General Stanley McChrystal, Commander of the International Security Assistance Force and U.S. Forces Afghanistan, included his conclusion that a successful counterinsurgency strategy would require 500,000 troops and an additional five years of fighting.[23] During a speech at West Point in December 2009, President Obama approved an increase of 30,000 troops; a modest increase that has proven to be inadequate in providing security to the population not to mention those attempting to implement the instruments of civilian power operating within the operational environment.[24]

On March 20, 2003, a combined coalition invasion of Iraq began with ground forces from predominantly the United States, Great Britain, Australia supported by Iraqi Kurdish Peshmerga. Another forty countries participated by providing equipment,

---

[21] Gary Berntsen and Ralph Pezzulla, Jawbreaker: The Attack on Bin Laden and AL Qaeda: A Personal Account by the CIA's Field Commander, (New York: Crowne Publishers, 2005), 106.

[22] Steve Coll, Ghost Wars: The Secret History of the CIA, Afghanistan, and Bin Laden, from the Soviet Invasion to September 10, 2001, (New York: Penguin Press, 2004), 214.

[23] Tom Andrews, "Classified McChrystal Report: 500,000 Troops Will Be Required Over Five Years in Afghanistan," Huffingtonpost (24 September 2009).

[24] Obama, 3.

services, Special Forces, and security personnel. The estimated total number of forces for the offensive was around 400,000.[25] The invasion was a quick and decisive operation encountering brief moments of major resistance, though not entirely what U.S. forces expected. "The Iraqi regime had prepared to fight both a conventional and irregular war at the same time, conceding territory when faced with superior conventional forces, largely armored, but launching smaller scale attacks in the rear using fighters dressed in civilian and paramilitary clothes."[26] This achieved some temporary successes and created unexpected challenges for the invading forces, especially the U.S. military.[27] On May 1, 2003, President Bush declared mission accomplished, announcing victory over the Iraqi conventional forces. Deemed an initial success, the conflict would move along the spectrum of conflict from general war to insurgency, which continues today.

Not unlike McChrystal in Afghanistan, General Erik Shinseki, Chief of Staff of the Army, "clashed with Secretary Rumsfeld during the planning of the war in Iraq over how many troops the U.S. would need for the postwar occupation of that country. Shinseki testified to the U.S. Senate that 'something in the order of several hundred thousand soldiers' would probably be required for postwar Iraq."[28] The scope and size of the forces General Shinseki desired were never approved, and the insurgency thrived. On June 30, 2009, seven years after his testimony, a permissive environment in Iraq was declared and a transfer of security to Iraqi forces occurred with the signing of U.S./Iraq

---

[25] E.J. Degen, Gregory Fontenot, and David Tohn, *On Point: The United States Army in Operation Iraqi Freedom*, (Fort Leavenworth, Kansas: Combat Studies Institute Press, 2004), xxvi.

[26] Ibid., xxvii.

[27] Ibid., xxvii.

[28] Senate Armed Services Committee, General Eric Shinseki testimony (February 25, 2003).

Security Forces Agreement (SFA).[29] Similar to President Bush's declaration that major combat operations in Iraq were completed, the SFA has also proven to be premature, with vehicle borne improvised explosive devices and homicide bombers continuing to disrupt civilian led operations throughout Iraq creating an unstable peace and definitely not a permissive environment.

Following WWII, there were over 4.5 million U.S. soldiers providing security to not only the population of Germany, but also to the U.S. government civilians and public and private organizations that were working to restore the basics of government: civil security, essential services, and rule of law.[30] Contrast this with Afghanistan and Iraq, where military leaders like Generals McChrystal and Shinseki requested additional numbers of forces to accomplish the stability mission and were subsequently denied or under resourced. The operational environments in both countries continue to be relatively non-permissive and unsuitable for civilian personnel working to forward national interests; the personal risk remains too high for many to assume. Today's war fighting paradigm must be considered when applying the whole-of-government approach to achieve national security interests.

Conclusion

Recent experiences in combat have shaped the desire for a collaborative and coordinated strategy with adequate resource implementation that will be utilized to achieve U.S. national interests in the future, capable of spanning the entire spectrum of

---

[29] Jason Coats and Mike Ryan, "The U.S./Iraq Security Agreement," *Military Review*, (September/October 2009): 48-53.

[30] Earl F. Ziemke, *The U.S. Army in the Occupation of Germany, 1944-1946*, (Washington D.C.: Center for Military History, 1975), 275.

conflict, from stable peace to general war.[31] The integration of resources required, applied with the appropriate ways to meet national interests, is the whole-of-government approach to national security strategy.

The whole-of-government approach "is derived from a thorough assessment of the strategic environment and *how* to advance our national interests within it".[32] National security professionals must have a firm grasp on this ever evolving strategic environment and how to effectively and efficiently utilize the instruments of national power within it. Informed by our current war fighting paradigm and understanding that the whole-of-government approach is to be utilized across the entire spectrum of conflict, the next chapter will review the specified direction our national leaders have provided our government.

---

[31] Operations, 2-1.

[32] National Military Strategy, 23.

CHAPTER 2:
THE GREAT STRENGTH OF OUR NATION

To attain our vital national interests, President Obama desires a harmonious, holistic approach, Secretary of Defense Gates speaks of a new jointness, Secretary of State Clinton calls for civilian power to complement military power, and Chairman Mullen envisions a whole-of-nation strategy. However different our national leaders may articulate the ways to employ our means to achieve our ends, their shared vision of a whole-of-government approach as the strategy is evident. This chapter will review their vision, as manifested in our national security documents, in detail.

National Security Strategy (NSS) 2010

General George Patton in 1941 understood the balance required by each element of military power to achieve victory. "To get the harmony in music each instrument must support the others. To get harmony in battle, each weapon must support the other. Team play wins."[1] During a speech at West Point on December 1, 2009, President Obama spoke about a nation out of balance— a nation failing "to appreciate the connection between our national security and our economy."[2] The balance which the President described is the relationship between our national ends, ways, and means. The President recognized that a valid strategy must achieve an appropriate balance of ends, ways, and means or its success will be at risk; in this case, achieving our vital national interests. While describing the way forward in Afghanistan, the President suggested that an imbalance in the ends, ways, and means had occurred and, consequently, contributed to

---

[1] United States Department of the Army, FM 3-09.31: Tactics, Techniques, and Procedures for Fire Support For the Combined Arms Commander, (Washington, D. C., 2002), 1-1.

[2] Obama, 2.

the current economic crisis in our nation. In the NSS, President Obama takes General Patton a step further by acknowledging that this balance is also required between each instrument of national power to effectively implement national strategy.[3] This harmony is the President's balanced strategy, the implementation of a whole-of-government approach where each instrument of power supports and complements the other.

The President's grasp of how to achieve our national strategy is influenced by his analysis of our current wars— "we can't count on military might alone."[4] To succeed, the United States must update, balance, and integrate all the tools of national power. The document the President utilizes to articulate this desire to achieve a balanced approach to the integration of the instruments of national power is the NSS. The NSS is a comprehensive articulation of the President's national security strategic approach and priorities for advancing American interests, including the security of the American people, a growing U.S. economy, support for our values, and an international order that can address 21st century challenges.[5]

> We must build and integrate the capabilities that can advance our interests, and the interests we share with other countries and peoples. Our military must be complemented by diplomats, development experts; and intelligence and law enforcement that can unravel plots, strengthen justice systems, and work seamlessly with other countries.[6]

He further expands upon the means to meet the strategy by including the private sector, nongovernmental organizations, and citizens.[7] The President recognizes that the

---

[3] National Security Strategy, 8.

[4] Obama, 3.

[5] National Security Strategy, 7.

[6] Ibid., 0.

[7] Ibid., 16.

greatest asset of America is our people— "the troops and civilians serving within our government; businesses, foundations, and educational institutions that operate around the globe; and citizens who possess the dynamism, drive, and diversity to thrive in a world that has grown smaller."[8]

"The United States and the international community cannot shy away from the difficult task of pursuing stabilization in conflict and post-conflict environments. In countries like Iraq and Afghanistan, building the capacity necessary for security, economic growth, and good governance is the only path to long term peace and security."[9] As the President acknowledged during his speech at West Point, our nation is out of balance and the risk is unacceptable.[10] To achieve the President's harmony and match our instruments of national power against our vital national interests, a whole-of-government approach is specifically directed.

National Defense Strategy (NDS) 2008

Secretary of Defense Robert Gate's NDS summarizes how the DoD supports the President's NSS and informs the National Military Strategy (NMS) and other strategy documents, building on lessons learned and insights from previous operations, specifically Iraq and Afghanistan in this case, and strategic reviews such as the Quadrennial Defense Review (QDR) 2006.[11] The NDS describes the environment as challenges ranging from violent transnational extremists networks, hostile states armed with WMD, rising regional powers, space and cyber threats, natural and pandemic

---

[8] National Security Strategy, 5.

[9] Ibid., 14-15.

[10] Ibid., 26.

[11] Jim Garomone, "Balance at Heart of New Defense Strategy," *Small Wars Journal* (July 31, 2008): 22.

disasters, and growing competition for resources. The DoD approach to meet these challenges is described as a new jointness— "our efforts require a unified approach to both planning and implementing policy. Iraq and Afghanistan remind us that military success alone is insufficient to achieve victory."[12]

The new jointness predates whole-of-government and desires to not only strengthen the military instrument of power but also reinvigorate other important elements of national power and develop the capability to integrate, tailor, and apply these tools as needed. We must tap the full strength of America and its people.[13] Secretary Gates directs the DoD to institutionalize and retain recently developed capabilities, such as long-term reconstruction, development, and governance. Describing these capabilities as a burden, he acknowledges that the DoD is no replacement for civilian involvement and expertise. "The United States must improve its ability to deploy civilian expertise rapidly."[14] Having permanent civilian capabilities available and using them early could also make it less likely that military forces will need to be deployed in the first place. A whole-of-government approach is only possible when every government department and agency understands the core competencies, roles, missions, and capabilities of its partners and works together to achieve common goals.[15]

Expounding upon the NDS, Secretary Gates describes a growing imbalance within our national security apparatus, with the response to challenges being uneven between the military and civilian elements of national power. "The problem is not will, it

---

[12] National Defense Strategy, 17.

[13] Ibid., 22.

[14] Ibid., 18.

[15] Ibid., 19.

is capacity"[16] Gates warns that even a better-funded DoS will not rid future military commanders from the burden of conducting the tasks that are better suited for civilians. "To truly achieve victory as Clausewitz defined it to attain a political objective, the U.S. needs a military whose ability to kick down the door is matched by its ability to clean up the mess and even rebuild the house afterward."[17]

National Military Strategy (NMS) 2011

Following President Obama's release of the NSS, Admiral Mullen expanded on the growing realization that to achieve our vital interests the strength of a nation would be required. Describing this, he pulled from a famous quote from General Omar Bradley that "battles are won by the infantry, the armor, the artillery, and air teams, by soldiers living in the rains and huddling in the snow. But wars are won by the great strength of a nation— the soldier and the civilian working together."[18] In the October 2010 Joint Forces Quarterly, the Chairman coined a new axiom for the strength of our nation applied to achieving vital national interests, the whole-of-nation approach. The Chairman reinforces President Obama's belief that the implementation of the instruments of national power is out of balance and that "U.S. foreign policy is still too dominated by the military. As President Obama noted in his West Point speech announcing his strategy for Afghanistan, we can't count on military might alone."[19]

---

[16] Robert M. Gates, "A Balanced Strategy: Reprogramming the Pentagon for a New Age," *DISAM Journal of International Security Assistance Management* 31(March 2009): 12.

[17] Ibid., 12.

[18] United States Department of the Army, *Pamphlet 600-65, Leadership Statements and Quotes* (Washington: U.S. Government Printing Office, November 1985), 4.

[19] Mike Mullen, "Working Together: Modern Challenges Need "Whole of Nation" Effort," *Joint Forces Quarterly* 59 (October 2010): 2.

The Chairman explains how diplomacy and defense must complement each other by working together rather than sequentially as one fails. He argues "that in future struggles that involve counterinsurgency and asymmetric warfare, we should commit our troops only when other instruments of national power and our allies are ready to engage as well."[20] The Weinberger Doctrine of the 1990s directed that once it was determined that vital national interests were at stake, "then we had to commit, as a last resort, not just token forces to provide an American presence, but enough forces to win and win overwhelmingly."[21] Comparably, the Mullen Doctrine desires overwhelming national power, not just the military instrument, but the whole of nation, prior to engaging our adversaries. The Chairman, however, has doubts about the implementation of this approach. He is concerned about "generating civilian capacity in a war zone for agency employees who had no expectation that they would serve in such a capacity."[22]

Informed by the NSS and the QDR, Admiral Mullen issued the first NMS in seven years in 2011. The purpose of the NMS is to provide the ways and means by which our military will advance our enduring national interests. In the Chairman's one page introduction to the document, he once again shares his vision of how "military power is most effective when employed in support and in concert with other elements of power as part of whole-of-nation approaches to foreign policy."[23] Military power alone is insufficient to fully address the complex security challenges we face. A whole-of-nation approach that utilizes the military to sustain regional partnership and complement

---

[20] Mullen, 2.

[21] Caspar Weinberger, *Fighting for Peace: Seven Critical Years in the Pentagon,* (New York: Warner Books, 1990), 160.

[22] Mullen, 3.

[23] National Military Strategy, 1.

economic development, governance, and rule of law must be shaped. "Military power and our nation's other instruments of statecraft are more effective when applied in concert. Trends in the strategic environment do not suggest this will change."[24]

Admiral Mullen directs the Joint Force to "support whole-of-nation deterrence approaches that blend economic, diplomatic, and military tools to influence adversary behavior."[25] The service chiefs, combatant commanders, and the entirety of the military will partner with other U.S. government agencies to actively pursue theater security cooperation. "We seek to facilitate interagency and enable international interoperability before crises occur. Preparation is indispensable when conditions demand collaboration."[26] The military must be the catalyst to facilitate and enable civilian power integration.

Quadrennial Defense Review (QDR) 2010

The QDR is congressionally mandated and instructs the DoD to review strategy, programs, and resources. Specifically, the QDR is expected to delineate a national defense strategy consistent with the most recent NSS by defining force structure, modernization plans, and a budget plan allowing the military to successfully execute the full range of missions within that strategy.[27] Consider the report a military back brief from the Secretary of Defense and CJCS to Congress detailing the military's ability to successfully execute specified missions as directed by the President within the forecasted budget plan and within acceptable risk. The QDR is the most succinct explanation as to

---

[24] National Military Strategy, 5.

[25] Ibid., 8.

[26] Ibid., 15.

[27] United States Department of Defense, *Quadrennial Defense Review Report* (Washington D.C., 2010), iii.

how the military will balance national interests, the ways to achieve those interests, and the resources available within the strategic environment while assuming low to moderate risk.

In the 2010 QDR, Secretary Gates is very clear that "preventing the rise of threats to U.S. interests requires the integrated use of diplomacy, development, and defense, along with intelligence, law enforcement, and economic tools of statecraft, to help build the capacity of partners to maintain and promote stability."[28] He sees the future strategic environment as providing our forces an opportunity to transition to a phase of reduced demanding sustained operations. This change in the military's current obligations will allow the DoD "to undertake a broader and deeper range of prevent-and-deter missions, acting wherever possible as part of a whole-of-government approach and in concert with allies and partners."[29] Acting wherever possible demonstrates the Secretary's belief that there will be times when the DoD must act alone to implement the whole-of-government approach.

"U.S. ground forces will remain capable of full-spectrum operations, with continued focus on capabilities to conduct effective and sustained counterinsurgency, stability, and counterterrorist operations alone and in concert with partners."[30] Recognizing the requirement for the whole-of-government approach as an appropriate strategy, Secretary Gates makes it clear to Congress that the DoD will be prepared to execute the mission with or without the rest of the interagency or partners; and, at the

---

[28] Quadrennial Defense Review, v.

[29] Ibid., vi.

[30] Ibid., x.

same time, "remains committed to further improving a whole-of-government approach to national security challenges."[31]

The First Quadrennial Diplomacy and Development Review (QDDR) 2010

The QDDR "follows in the footsteps of the QDR in taking a comprehensive look at how we can spend our resources most efficiently, how we can achieve our priorities most effectively, what we should be doing differently, and how we should prepare ourselves for the world ahead."[32] While serving as a Senator on the Armed Services Committee, Secretary of State Clinton was exposed to what a valuable tool the QDR was for Congress. Similarly, Secretary Clinton understands that a QDDR would not only provide the national leadership with the how DoS would balance the ends, ways, and means within acceptable risk; but also would provide very clear guidance to subordinates prioritizing objectives and resources. The QDDR would be the mechanism to provide a strategic plan for the DoS.

Much like Secretary Gates' new jointness and Admiral Mullen's whole-of-nation, Secretary Clinton introduces the comprehensive term *civilian power*.

> Civilian power is the combined force of women and men across the U.S. government who are practicing diplomacy, implementing development projects, strengthening alliances and partnerships, preventing and responding to crises and conflict, and advancing America's core interests: security, prosperity, universal values—especially democracy and human rights—and a just international order. It is the civilian side of the government working as one, just as our military services work together as a unified force.[33]

---

[31] Quadrennial Defense Review, xi.

[32] United States Department of State, *The First Quadrennial Diplomacy and Development Review* (Washington D.C., 2010), 2.

[33] Ibid., 2.

Secretary Clinton simplifies the instruments of national power as described by the President in the NSS to just two— civilian power and military power. In the QDDR, she assumes the lead in unifying the other government agencies and departments and public and private partners under the DoS. Civilian power is not limited to DoS alone, but all civilian agencies that engage in international activity from "energy diplomacy, disease prevention, police training, trade promotion, and many other areas."[34]

A distinct difference from the whole-of-nation approach as describe by Admiral Mullen and Secretary Clinton's interpretation of the whole-of-government approach is the role that public and private partners will play in achieving our national interests. Admiral Mullen believes that the President wants us to influence and encourage public and private enterprises when and wherever possible to assist or at times act independently, while Secretary Clinton sees the use of private contractors as a last resort. The DoS must "fundamentally change our management approach by turning to the expertise of other federal agencies where appropriate— *before* engaging private contractors. This will help all federal agencies build lasting relationships with foreign counterparts and reduce our reliance on contractors."[35]

Even with the reluctance to use private and public organizations as a replacement to federal employees, Secretary Clinton recognizes that "today, non-state actors— from NGOs, religious groups, and multinational corporations to international cartels and terrorist networks— are playing an ever-greater role in international affairs."[36] To incorporate these actors into civilian power, the Secretary realizes that she must first fix

---

[34] Quadrennial Diplomacy and Development Review, 2.

[35] Ibid., 6.

[36] Ibid., 8.

her own house. "Our civilian capabilities have largely been ad hoc and poorly integrated with those of other federal agencies and partner nations. We must learn from our experiences as we define the civilian mission and give our people the training, tools, and structures they need."[37]

Secretary Clinton recognizes that "although traditional diplomacy will always be critical to advancing the United States' agenda, it is not enough. The State Department is broadening the way it conceives diplomacy as well as the roles and responsibilities of its practitioners."[38] The central theme of the QDDR is clear, that not only must State and USAID work better together, but cooperation across the whole-of-government must take place. To facilitate this cooperation, Secretary Clinton *pins the rose* on the DoS.[39]

Conclusion

Admiral Mullen said recently, "Just because a soldier can do it, that doesn't mean a soldier should do it."[40] As seen by our national narratives, our President and senior leaders fully acknowledge that the best strategy to achieve our vital interests is a whole-of-government approach that is inclusive of an ever expanding list of instruments of national power. "With the right balance of civilian and military power, the United States can advance its interests and values, lead and support other nations in solving global problems, and forge strong diplomatic and development partnerships with traditional allies and newly emerging powers."[41] This chapter provides a brief narrative of the

---

[37] Quadrennial Diplomacy and Development Review, 13.

[38] Clinton, 11.

[39] Quadrennial Diplomacy and Development Review, 19.

[40] Kevin Baron, "White House Struggling to Budge Congress on Civilian Aid for Wars," *Stars and Stripes*, December 6, 2010.

[41] Clinton, 11.

strategy our national leaders conclude must be implemented to achieve our vital interests, the whole-of-government approach. The next chapter will discuss what has actually been done to meet this strategy; will the strong rhetoric be supported by actions that can truly relieve the DoD from missions that should be done by civilians or will our accomplishment of national interests fall on the shoulders of soldiers alone?

CHAPTER 3:
FALLING SHORT

Well, you know, we went in, and we expected a fight; we got a fight. And then I always expected that I'd look over my shoulder, and there would be battalions of nation-builders from the Office of Reconstruction and Humanitarian Assistance or someone from the Coalition Provincial Authority. I kept on looking around, and they didn't show up. Then I realized I'd have to be doing some of that.[1]

Anonymous Soldier, Operation Iraqi Freedom

If current initiatives by the U.S. government is the way forward, then *doing some of that* will remain a pickup game for our nation and unfortunately our military. A review of the implementation of DoD Directive 3000.05, which will be discussed in greater detail in this chapter, concluded

> that immensely insufficient capacity in the government outside of DoD will remain a problem in the conduct of effective stability operations in dangerous environments. Promoting increased deployable civilian capacity must remain a top DoD priority, but the process will take years, if not decades, and require revolutionary Congressional action with respect to budgets and authorities. Hardly any new deployable civilian capacity in other departments and agencies has been created in the last several years despite Presidential requests, National Security Presidential Directives, and Defense Department urging.[2]

This chapter will discuss current initiatives that have been enacted to create the cooperative and collaborative whole-of-government approach as envisioned by our national leaders. This chapter will also discuss shortfalls in meeting these expectations.

Project on National Security Reform

The National Defense Authorization Act for Fiscal Year 2008 called for a study to be conducted of the national security interagency system by an independent, non-profit, non-partisan organization. The study was titled the Project on National Security Reform

---

[1] Thomas P.M. Barnett, *Great Powers*, (New York: G.P. Putnam's Sons, 2009), 261.

[2] United States Department of Defense, *Interim Progress Report on DoD Directive 3000.05*, (Washington D.C.: Office for the Undersecretary of Defense for Policy, August 2006), 18.

(PNSR) and attempted to indentify risks and misalignments of the current system. The study focused on the defense of the United States and concluded that the current national security system does not allow integration between national, regional, multilateral, and state and local agencies.[3] Even though the PNSR focused on national defense, the conclusions are applicable to achieving vital national interests within the international environment.

The study identified the two primary reasons for this unacceptable risk in the national security system. "First, the system consists of autonomous organizations directly funded by Congress separately that focus on their respective goals and missions. Second, only the president has the authority to integrate across these autonomous agencies, but the president has no effective way to delegate his authority."[4] When dealing with disparate government agencies, the President's ability to command and control is hampered because of a lack of synergy. No central vision exists that builds unity of purpose and effort— goals, plans, and procedures are mismatched and not mutually supportive.

The system is unable to integrate or cross-level resources across government agencies to achieve national security objectives. "With the exception of the DoD, the individual organizations that make up the system do not have strong traditions of long-term planning. The yearly budget cycle encourages short-term thinking and spending and focuses on outputs rather than on outcomes."[5]

---

[3] Forging a New Shield, 3.

[4] Ibid., 208.

[5] Forging a New Shield, 205.

The review also provided four key recommendations to the national security

system. First, a multidimensional concept to address challenges, current and future, must

be created. Second, the integration of diverse skills and perspectives must happen.

Third, the budgeting and resource allocation of national means should be reapportioned;

and fourth, improve the planning and execution capability for potential future

contingencies.[6] "These four key principles assist in achieving horizontal and vertical

coordination to eliminate the tunnel vision of departmentalism by making better use of

scarce resources and creating synergies by bringing together all departments that

contribute to national security."[7] Simply put, the PNSR prescribes the whole-of-

government approach.

Department of Defense Instruction 3000.05

"DoD components have been explicitly directed to address and integrate stability

operations— related concepts and capabilities across a panorama of doctrine,

organization, training, material, leadership and education, personnel, and facilities

(DOTMLPF), and applicable exercises, strategies, and plans."[8] DoD Instruction 3000.05

clearly states that "many stability operations tasks are best performed by indigenous,

foreign, or U.S. civilian professionals". [9] However, as the Undersecretary of Defense for

Policy, Ms. Michele Flournoy concludes "many U.S. government agencies do not yet

have the capacity or the capability to respond to the degree necessary. Improving the

---

[6] Ibid., 200.

[7] Tom Christensen and Per Laegreid, "The Whole-of-Government Approach to Public Sector Reform," *Public Administration Review* 67, (November/December 2007): 1059-1066.

[8] D.H. Gurney, "Executive Summary," *Joint Forces Quarterly* 57 (2nd Quarter 2010): 7.

[9] DoD Instruction 3000.05, 2.

capacity of civilian agencies and integrating civilian and military activities to ensure unity of effort in such operations is critical."[10]

The Directive instructs DoD to conduct stability operations across the full spectrum of conflict and the continuum of military operations, obviously the scale and duration will vary. Additionally, the DoD will support other U. S. government agencies, foreign governments, and their security forces and international governmental organizations when directed. The DoD will also lead stability operations (establish civil security and control, restore essential services, protect and repair critical infrastructure, and deliver humanitarian assistance) until the capability and capacity exists in other government agencies to assume the lead. To meet this requirement, the DoD must build the structure to enable the deployment, integration, and utilization of appropriate civilian capabilities to conduct all types of operations across the full spectrum of conflict in an uncertain joint, interagency, intergovernmental, and multinational environment over an extended period.[11] The DoD must be the catalyst to force interagency integration.

Full Spectrum Mission Essential Task List

To conduct operations throughout the full spectrum of conflict as directed by DoD Directive 3000.05, the tasks that the military must train on must change. Instead of stability being delegated to civil affairs or support organizations, the total force must focus on the entire continuum of operations. To bring stability on par with offense and defense, the mission essential tasks must be adjusted. Paradoxically, "good leaders

---

[10] Michele Flournoy, "USG Civilian Capabilities," Office for the Undersecretary of Defense for Policy, http://policy.defense.gov/solic/psso/usgcapabilities.aspx (accessed February 28, 2011).

[11] United States Department of Defense, *Department of Defense Instruction Number 3000.05: Stability Operations*, (Washington D.C., September 16, 2009), 2.

understand that they cannot train on everything; therefore, they focus on training the most important tasks. Training a few tasks to standard is preferable to training more tasks below the standard."[12]

The Vice Chief of Staff of the Army, General Chiarelli, weighs in, "It is simply impossible to plan and train for every possible scenario our soldiers and their leaders may encounter within the complex reality of the contemporary operating environments."[13] The December 2008 version of Field Manual (FM) 7-0 discussed training in a post-9/11 world and the need to train units for full-spectrum operations in any operational environment, anywhere along the spectrum of conflict.[14] FM 7-0, however, indicated the training environment would tend to replicate *either* major combat operations or irregular warfare conditions rather than reflect the reality of a hybrid threat— a mix of conventional, irregular, terrorist and criminal elements. The manual also did not clearly reinforce that offense, defense, and stability operations will occur simultaneously and throughout the spectrum of conflict. Therefore, the Chief of Staff of the Army directed the Training and Doctrine Command to revise FM 7-0 to provide a single mission essential task list concept, based on the complete continuum of operations, to better address the strategic environment and simplify the training management process.[15] Even though the military has made an effort to adjust doctrine and training to meet the whole-of-government requirements, the DoD still falls short.

---

[12] United States Department of the Army, *FM 7-0: Training For Full Spectrum Operations*, (Washington, D.C., 2008), 2-46.

[13] Peter Chiarelli, "Training Full Spectrum, Less is More," *Army Magazine* (June 2009): 11.

[14] Training For Full Spectrum Operations, 2-48.

[15] Chiarelli, 12.

Irregular Warfare Roadmap

"The DoD has established an aggressive timeline for implementing approximately thirty tasks over the next year in order to improve our ability to conduct irregular warfare, known as the Irregular Warfare Roadmap. The focus of this roadmap is enhancing irregular warfare capabilities and capacity throughout the Department."[16] The roadmap emphasizes building partner capacity, creating educational and long-term training opportunities for officers, specifically in the areas of language skills and cultural knowledge, and a focus on fostering civil society and good governance in otherwise ungoverned areas. The roadmap was directed in the 2005 QDR and has since been expanded upon in the 2010 Joint Operating Concept (JOC).

The JOC comes closest in offering specific guidance in the implementation of DoD Instruction 3000.05 simply because the capabilities required to execute stability operations also reside within the core competencies of irregular warfare. The JOC acknowledges that the shortage of other government agencies will require the use of DoD personnel to fill the gaps in critical non-military skills in governance, essential service development, and rule of law. Additionally, the JOC directs the DoD to identify lessons learned and best practices from past irregular warfare operations and use these to be a catalyst for informing and building capabilities within other government agencies.[17]

DOD Falling Short

A progress report on the implementation of DoD Instruction 3000.05 concluded that the "DoD components have made progress in meeting the exigencies of ongoing

---

[16] Mario Mancuso, "Irregular Warfare Roadmap," *Special Operations Technology* Volume 9, Issue 1 (February 2011): 22.

[17] United States Department of Defense, Irregular Warfare: Countering Irregular Threats: Joint Operating Concept, Version 2.0 (17 May 2010), 36.

stability operations and the challenges identified in DoD Instruction 3000.05. This progress however, has been uneven, ad hoc, and incomplete. Continued support from senior leaders throughout DoD is required to drive and institutionalize the changes."[18] The report also stresses that "U.S. military forces shall be prepared to perform all tasks necessary to establish or maintain order when civilians cannot do so."[19] However, the continued reluctance of military leaders to properly address the *how* prevents our nation from effectively "maintaining or reestablishing a safe and secure environment, providing essential governmental services, emergency infrastructure reconstruction, and humanitarian relief" in stability operations.[20]

The DoD has inadequately emphasized the importance of stability operations tasks in virtually all critical DoD missions and must continue to "mitigate the negative effects of predictable gaps in civilian capacity by preparing U.S. military forces for likely stability operations tasks." [21] Publishing a directive, facilitating a discussion about mission essential tasks, and creating slight doctrinal changes falls short in the requirement to change the DOTMLPF across DoD.

National Security Presidential Directive-44 (NSPD-44)

In December 2005, President Bush issued a Presidential Directive designed to empower the Secretary of State to improve coordination, planning, and implementation for reconstruction and stabilization assistance for foreign states and regions at risk of, in,

---

[18] United States Department of Defense, *Report to Congress on the Implementation Progress of DoD 3000.05*, (Washington D.C.: April 1, 2007), 12.

[19] DoD Directive 3000.05, 2.

[20] Operations, 3-6.

[21] Report to Congress on the Implementation Progress of DoD 3000.05, 7.

or in transition from conflict or civil strife.[22] The intent was to expand capability and capacity within the civilian governmental instruments of power

> to enable the U.S. to help governments abroad exercise sovereignty over their own territories and to prevent those territories from being used as a base of operations or safe haven for extremists, terrorists, organized crime groups, or others who pose a threat to U.S. foreign policy, security, or economic interests.[23]

The Directive attempted to strengthen U.S. capacity to develop and implement integrated responses, coordinated with international and non-governmental partners "allowing for a unified national strategy for conflict transformation, rather than a collection of agency responses."[24]

NSPD-44 was an executive decision to bolster a whole-of-government response and is commonly referred to as the companion piece to DoD Directive 3000.05. NPSD-44 directs "the Secretary of State to coordinate and lead integrated U.S. Government efforts, involving all U.S. Departments and Agencies with relevant capabilities, to prepare, plan for, and conduct stabilization and reconstruction activities. The Secretary of State shall coordinate such efforts with the DoD to ensure harmonization with any planned or ongoing U.S. military operations across the spectrum of conflict."[25]

Additionally, NSPD-44 directs the DoS to be the supported government agency to coordinate and lead integrated U.S. efforts to conduct stabilization and reconstruction, with or without military forces. When the U.S. military is involved, the DoS shall

---

[22] Department of State Fact Sheet, "President Issues Directive to Improve the United States' Capacity to Manage Reconstruction and Stabilization Efforts," http://www.fas.org/irp/offdocs/nspd/nspd-44fs.html (accessed April 25, 2011).

[23] United States President Directive, "National Security Presidential Directive/NSPD-44," (December 7, 2005), 2.

[24] Ibid., 2.

[25] "National Security Presidential Directive," 2.

coordinate such efforts with the DoD to ensure synchronization with any planned or ongoing U.S. military operation across the full spectrum of conflict.[26] "The United States shall work with other countries and organizations, to anticipate state failure, avoid it whenever possible, and respond quickly and effectively when necessary and appropriate to promote peace, security, development, democratic practices, market economies, and the rule of law."[27]

NSPD-44 "calls on each agency to strengthen its capacity to respond to crises; mobilize expert staff; participate in deployed teams; and assist with planning, policy exercises, and training."[28] The burden is not solely the DoS's challenge, but clearly the directive is directed at all government agencies and departments. The Directive is also global in nature, directing all agencies to focus on our international partners. "There is unprecedented collaboration among international and non-governmental partners to build global capacity for conflict management. The Directive instructs U.S. agencies, with the DoS in the coordination lead, to work with these key partners on early warning, prevention, and conflict response."[29] As a supporting agency, the DoD has provided expertise and assistance to the DoS to ensure compliance under NSPD-44.

Coordinator for Reconstruction and Stabilization

To meet this increase in responsibility, NSPD-44 validated an organizational change within DoS and established the Coordinator for Reconstruction and Stabilization (S/CRS). S/CRS was directed to develop strategies and options for national leadership

---

[26] "President Issues Directive to Improve," 1.

[27] "National Security Presidential Directive," 5.

[28] Ibid., 7.

[29] "National Security Presidential Directive," 7.

while ensuring policy coordination and collaboration throughout all agencies and departments within the federal government.

"The S/CRS is the lead coordinator for reconstruction and stabilization activities with partners, international and regional organizations, and nongovernmental and private sector entities."[30] The S/CRS is to be predictive in nature, providing analysis of states at risk to mitigate or even prevent conflict. Additionally, S/CRS is self-critical and provides lessons learned to improve the whole-of-government strategy to reconstruction and stabilization.[31]

Civilian Response Corps

Over a decade of operational experience has underscored the need for a civilian field presence in the very first stages of a stabilization mission. S/CRS has been working with civilian agencies and the military to develop concepts for providing the U.S. with deployable civilian teams for stabilization that can embed with the military or operate independently.[32]

In accordance with NSPD-44, the DoS initiated a Civilian Response Corps (CRC) to become the diplomatic *boots on the ground*.

The CRC would provide immediately deployable teams of civilian technical experts, regardless of military involvement, to areas of concern.[33] These civilian technical experts exist throughout the federal government, and "in order to adequately address these complexities and leverage all available resources of the U.S. Government,

---

[30] Ibid., 14.

[31] Ibid., 15.

[32] Ibid., 25.

[33] "National Security Presidential Directive," 26.

the CRC is comprised of a partnership of eight departments and agencies from around the federal government."[34]

DoS Falling Short

NSPD-44 and the subsequent establishment of S/CRS "were positive steps to increasing interagency integration, but few resources have been allocated and little action has been taken to implement the Directive. DoD continues to support efforts within the executive and legislative branches to provide resources to its non-military partners."[35] Much like DoD, the civilian power stake holders have done little to meet any of the DOTMLPF requirements. Following are a few examples of falling short.

Funding is imperative to implement the civilian power initiatives as outlined in NSPD-44 and the QDDR; however, Congress has made it clear that resources will not be available. Florida Congresswoman Ileana Ros-Lehtinen (R-FL), the Chair of the House Foreign Affairs Committee, recently declared that her "job is to cut the State and foreign aid budgets."[36]

The current war fighting paradigm has also impacted the DoS budget. Because of non-permissive operational environments, the force protection budget for the DoS has gone from $200 million in 1998 to $2.3 billion today.[37] Essentially, embassies have become walled fortresses, isolating those within from host country population both

---

[34] Ibid., 26.

[35] Report to Congress on the Implementation Progress of DoD 3000.05, 20.

[36] Josh Rogin, "Ros-Lehtinen, My Mission is to Cut the State and Foreign Aid Budgets," *The Cable* (December 8, 2010).

[37] James Carafano, "Budgets and Threats: An Analysis of Strategic Priorities for Maritime Security," *The Heritage Foundation* 791 (June 16, 2003): 3.

physically and psychologically, totally secure *yet* totally useless.[38] Much of this may be necessary, but more risk must be accepted to achieve mission accomplishment. The only long term solution that might assure adequate resources for a substantially enhanced civilian national security role is a unified national security budget that incorporates military, intelligence, diplomacy, and development.

The sustainable recent gains in conflict and crisis response capacity are highly questionable and in jeopardy, especially with growing civilian demands in Iraq and Afghanistan as military force withdrawals proceed, and the transition to *civilian power in the lead* occurs. Today, twenty five percent of State Foreign Service Officers and ten percent of USAID staff are currently stationed in Iraq, Afghanistan, or Pakistan.[39] Additionally, USAID has transformed from a technically skilled organization focused on project development and implementation into a primarily contracting and grant-making organization. In 1970, there was more USAID staff in Vietnam than the worldwide total in 2008.[40]

The CRC now has about 131 active full time members and 1,040 stand-by members (federal employees and retirees who can be deployed on short notice), the current goal is to grow to 500 active and 1500 stand-by. The CRC has expanded to represent nine government agencies.[41] Not only is the CRC extremely small in size, the

---

[38] Andrea Mitchell, "Fortress America, New U.S. Embassy in Iraq Cloaked in Mystery," *New York Times* (April 14, 2006).

[39] Jacob J. Lew, *President's Proposal for the FY 2011 State Department Budget* (Washington D.C.: Deputy Secretary for Management and Resources, February 1, 2010), 1.

[40] Kathryn Blakeman and William B. Skelton, *2008-2009 Annual Edition: Journal for the Study of Peace and Conflict* (Wisconsin Institute for Peace and Conflict Studies: January, 2008): 18.

[41] United States Department of State, "Civil Response Corps," Office for Reconstruction and Stabilization, http://www.crs.state.gov/index.cfm?fuseaction=public.display&shortcut=4QRB (accessed February 28, 2011).

CRC is voluntary, so no matter how vital the national interest or requirement to respond, the member can make the decision to personally reject any deployment.

Congress: Skelton-Davis (INSPEAD) System Act

DoD Instruction 1120.11 provides guidance to all of the services on military manpower, programming, and accounting. The instruction directs the services to establish an account that incorporates the following categories of trainees, transients, holdees, and students (TTHS) representing soldiers not assigned to units.[42] TTHS allows the military services to account for personnel not assigned to units within their respective force structure. The instruction is a critical element in allowing the services to train and educate leaders, supply ready soldiers to perform their combat mission, and provides for the transition of soldiers to citizens. Without such a tool, training, education, and leader development would suffer.[43] The requisite tool in our government's civilian agencies does not exist and continues to be a barrier to effective interagency participation within national security operations.

Civilian personnel within our government agencies are often ill-prepared and unqualified to effectively participate in the planning and execution of national security operations. This is more greatly exasperated in agencies that do not work within the national security framework on a daily basis. To tackle this deficit, the Interagency National Security Professional Education, Administration, and Development (INSPEAD) System Act of 2010 was introduced by the Chairman of the House Armed Services

---

[42] United States Department of Defense, Department of Defense Instruction 1120.11: Programming and Accounting for Active Military Manpower (Washington D.C.: October 30, 2007), 12.

[43] Scott T. Nestler, "TTHS Is Not a Four-Letter Word," *Institute for Land Warfare* Essay 04-7W (Association of the United States Army: November 2004), 4.

Committee, Representative Ike Skelton (D-MO), along with Representative Geoff Davis (R-KY). "This is an attempt by law, not by regulation but by law, to change the culture of the national security system so that the right hand knows what the left hand is doing."[44]

The intent of the Act is to provide education, training, and interagency assignments to select personnel across the federal government developing an interagency national security professional.[45]

> The new bill incorporates many of the recommendations that have been developed from the Project on National Security Reform (PNSR) studies in the past three years, including the "Forging a New Shield" study that was released in December 2008. The bill also incorporates a number of recommendations that are being developed through the 2010 Quadrennial Defense Review (QDR) and the 2010 Quadrennial Diplomacy and Development Review(QDDR) to advance the "comprehensive approach" for national security issues.[46]

The bill would require senior level interagency security professionals seeking positions of increased authority and promotion to meet specific education, training, and experience requirements.[47] The bill also requires funding to be authorized to create the program and necessary structures for implementation of the system.

---

[44] Jen Kohl, "Skelton, Davis Introduce Groundbreaking Interagency Reform Legislation," *CNN Politics* (September 30, 2010), http://articles.cnn.com/2010-09-30/politics/house.security.bill_1_skelton-national-security-collaboration?_s=PM:POLITICS (accessed February 28, 2011).

[45] Geoff Davis, "Legislation Targeted at Reforming National Security, *AUSA News* (February 1, 2011).

[46] Jack Kem, "INSPEAD: Going Beyond Goldwater-Nichols," *Combined Arms Center Blog* (Fort Leavenworth, Kansas: October 2, 2010): 1.

[47] Ibid., 1.

Congress Falling Short

INSPEAD is a first step, but falls woefully short of expectations of a revolutionary Goldwater-Nichols Act for civilian power. The Act has seen little movement within Congress, and the failure of Senator Skelton to win re-election only exacerbates its progress. Hailed as the answer to improving security collaboration, the Act only addresses leader development opportunities and none of the other DOTMLPF categories.[48]

Conclusion

DoD Directive 3000.05 is just one example of the numerous articulated directives for the military instrument of power to elevate stability operations to the same proficiency as equivalent combat operations allowing the military to be integrated into the whole-of-government approach to national security. Over the past several years, U.S. Government agencies have also been revising their thinking on the whole-of-government approach. Despite recent specified guidance and directives from the national level leadership, our nation still falls short. With the predominantly non-permissive complex environments preventing civilians from assisting in stability operations and the lack of a Goldwater-Nichols equivalent Act to build other government agency capacity and capability, the DoD continues to be the only department or agency capable of carrying out the whole-of-government approach across the full spectrum of conflict.

The requirement for a whole-of-government approach and the *how* to resource and prepare the instruments of power to best be balanced and integrated has been addressed, but our government falls short with any actual action. Continued baseless

---

[48] Kohl, 22.

rhetoric forces the DoD to be prepared to execute the whole-of-government approach alone or with little support from the other government agencies and departments. This next chapter will review historical cases where the U.S. military executed the whole-of-government approach and will attempt to provide possible analysis that can be used for recommendations for our nation in the future.

CHAPTER 4:
FAILURE TO LEARN- INFORMING THE FUTURE

The events which happened in the past… (human nature being what it is) will at some time or other and in much the same way be repeated in the future. [1]

Thucydides

The United States liberated Kuwait in 1991. In 1992, U.S. troops went into Somalia, in 1994 into Haiti, in 1995 into Bosnia, in 1999 into Kosovo, and in 2001 into Afghanistan. Six of these seven societies were Muslim. Thus by the time U.S. troops entered Iraq, no country in the world had more modern experience in nation-building than the United States, and no Western military had more extensive recent practice operating within Muslim societies.[2] Unfortunately, our nation failed to properly learn from these experiences. This chapter offers an analysis of two conflicts, WWII and Vietnam, where the military attempted the whole-of-government approach. The objective is to not only provide a historical overview but to also provide a rudimentary examination that can inform the future of U.S. government engagement throughout the full spectrum of conflict and across the entire operational continuum.

Occupations of Germany and Japan during WWII

General Eisenhower in North Africa in 1942 summed up the feelings of most military professionals during sustained conflict, "The sooner I can get rid of these questions that are outside the military in scope, the happier I will be! Sometimes I think I live ten years each week, of which at least nine are absorbed

---

[1] Thucydides, *The History of the Peloponnesian War*, translated by Rex Warner, (London: Penguin Books, 1954), 48.

[2] Dobbins, xviii.

in political and economic matters."[3] Much to his surprise and dismay, General

Eisenhower never got rid of these questions that were outside the scope of the

military.

The U.S. military was no stranger to stability operations entering WWII;

in fact, our forces were committed to Germany for several years following WWI.

> The U.S. Army and government had not really accepted the administration of civil government in occupied enemy territory as a legitimate military function after the Mexican War, Civil War, or Spanish-American War, and the officer in charge of civil affairs for the U.S. military government in the Rhineland after World War I lamented that the American army of occupation lacked both training and organization to perform its duties.[4]

Equipped with the lessons learned from WWI, however different in scope, the Army

prepared for future governmental challenges that they would be facing after WWII.

Within months following the attack on Pearl Harbor by Japan, the Army Chief of Staff,

General George C. Marshall began preparation for occupation and reconstruction duties.

These responsibilities covered not only military action, but also political, economic, and

social challenges.

School of Military Governance

Armed with experience and doctrine, the military remained reluctant to prepare

for the inevitable occupations of friendly and enemy territory during World War II. In

fact, President Roosevelt's view of military government as strange and abhorrent was

---

[3] Harry L. Coles and Albert K. Weinberg, *Civil Affairs: Soldiers Become Governors*, (Washington DC: United States Army Center of Military History, 1992), 3.

[4] Conrad C. Crane and W. Andrew Terrill, "Reconstructing Iraq: Insights, Challenges, and Missions for Military Forces in a Post-Conflict Scenario," Monograph (Strategic Studies Institute: February 2003): 7.

consistent with General Eisenhower's desire to turn responsibility over to civilian authorities as soon as possible.[5]

"Following WWI, governance was viewed by most officers exclusively as a function related to military law, however by the mid 1930s this conventional wisdom began to change, expanding the definition to include activities related to civil administration."[6] In October 1940, the Army publishing of Field Manual 27-10, *The Rules of Land Warfare*, and Field Manual 27-5, *Military Government*, influenced "the idea of creating a special school to educate uniformed personnel in military government gained any real momentum."[7]

Concerned that U.S. forces may be left with no civil government in place throughout several occupied territories, U.S. military officials turned their attention to the British who had already been faced with occupations of conquered nations— Eritrea, Cyrenaica, and Italian Somaliland. At St. John's College in Cambridge, the British War Office established what would become the first school for military officers focusing on governance.[8] The U.S. Army sent several officers to the British course and their after action report confirmed that the time had come to establish a similar school. The U.S. Army School of Military Government was established at the University of Virginia in Charlottesville on April 2, 1942.[9]

---

[5] Harry L. Colas and Albert K. Weinberg, *Civil Affairs: Soldiers Become Governors,* (Washington D.C.: United States Army Center for Military History, 1964), 88.

[6] Ziemke, 3.

[7] Brent C. Bankus and James Kievit, "The Army and Marines and Military Government," *Small Wars Journal* online, http://smallwarsjournal.com/documents/bankuskievit.doc (accessed 28 February 2011).

[8] Ziemke, 4-5.

[9] Bankus, 5.

"The makeup of the first class consisted of younger officers of talent and ability and with backgrounds more or less equally distributed among the special fields, engineers (electrical, civil and sanitation), accountants, lawyers, economists, sociologists and the like."[10] Local and state principles of public administration including public finance, health, and sanitation; communications; utilities and public works; education, public safety, public welfare and economic problems; made up the curriculum.[11] By November 1943, the School of Military Government consisted of eleven satellite campuses— Boston, Chicago, Harvard, Michigan, Northwestern, Pittsburgh, Princeton, Stanford, Western Reserve, Wisconsin, and Yale.[12]

As the School of Military Government expanded to meet the increasing requirements with each Allied victory, the initial graduates were already performing their duties in Sicily and Italy.[13] "As the requirement to create additional military organizations for the differing theaters decreased, the various military government education programs were terminated. But their alumni would continue to play significant roles during the eminently successful post-WWII occupations of Germany and Japan."[14] The success of these missions can also be attributed to the superior leadership of General Douglas MacArthur in Japan and General Lucius Clay in Germany.

---

[10] Coles, 10.

[11] Ibid., 12.

[12] John Lada, *Civil Affairs/Military Government Public Health Activities, Preventive Medicine in World War II*, Volume VII (Washington D.C.: Office of the Surgeon General United States Army, 1976), 31.

[13] Ziemke, 22.

[14] Bankus, 17.

Unity of Command

General Clay, an Army engineer and expert at reconstruction, was selected by President Roosevelt to take charge of the American sector in southern occupied Germany, assuming his official duties under the leadership of President Truman.[15] The military government command was entirely in tactical channels facilitating the transition from combat operations to that of stability. In Japan, General MacArthur was given complete authority for postwar occupation, even authority over the media and Japanese educational and social policy.[16]

Soldiers as Diplomats

As U.S. soldiers entered Germany on September 11, 1944, units specifically prepared to conduct the governance mission trailed their advance. These units were trained in the reestablishment of civil security, essential services, and rule of law. "Within days of full occupation, U.S. civil affairs units sent detachments into every town, establishing security and U.S. authority in each population center within the U.S. sector."[17] On August 15, 1945, only days after Emperor Hirohito surrendered, an almost identical situation as in Germany occurred in Japan. General Douglas MacArthur arrived in Tokyo and set up his command. "He sent troops and civil affairs officers on rounds of motorcycle diplomacy throughout the country to establish security and to explain U.S. intentions while managing local expectations of the military government."[18]

---

[15] Ray Salvatore Jennings, *The Road Ahead*, (Washington D.C.: United States Institute for Peace, April 2003), 5.

[16] Earl Frederick Ziemke, *The U.S. Army in the Occupation of Germany, 1944-1946*, (Washington D.C.: U.S. Government Printing Office, 1975), 12.

[17] Jennings, 5.

[18] Ibid., 6.

In Germany and Japan, combat troops transitioned from their primary military specialty and began working governance issues. "Soldiers were issued handbooks, detailing the rules of engagement with local populations as well as the appropriate responses to administrative dilemmas, the structure of local governance institutions, methods to disarm local police, and the manner in which civil disturbances should be settled."[19]

Vietnam

The Vietnam War provides an opportunity for an in-depth analysis that spans the full spectrum of conflict across the continuum of operations. Attempting to bring stability to South Vietnam, our government attempted to integrate all the instruments of national power in a conventional fight with the North Vietnamese Army (NVA) and a counterinsurgency campaign. Each effort suffered from numerous challenges that prevented ultimate success; however, several programs were successful and can inform the future. Two of these successful aspects from the Vietnam War, Civil Operations and Rural Development Support (CORDS) and Combined Action Platoons (CAP) can highlight opportunities for conflicts today and in the future.

Civil Operations and Rural Development Support (CORDS)

In January 1966, General William Westmoreland, Commander of the Military Assistance Command-Vietnam (MACV) wrote, "It is abundantly clear that all political, military, economic, and security (police) programs must be completely integrated in order to attain any kind of success in a country which has been greatly weakened by

---

[19] Jennings, 6.

prolonged conflict."[20] In May 1967, a new organization, the Civil Operations and

Revolutionary Development Support (CORDS) program was established to coordinate

the U.S. civil and military pacification programs as directed by General Westmorland.

Unity of Command

A key lesson learned from pacification operations in Vietnam is that unity of

command is paramount to insure that all agencies involved are cooperating and working

toward the same goal. The development of the CORDS program during the Vietnam

War offers a good example of how to establish a chain of command incorporating civilian

and military agencies into a focused effort.

CORDS was a unique program that involved a civil-military structure, "placing

the disjointed and ineffective civilian pacification programs under the military. This was

accomplished at the insistence of President Johnson, who took an active interest in seeing

the pacification process function smoothly under a single manager: Westmoreland."[21]

CORDS pulled together all the various U.S. military and civilian agencies involved in the

pacification effort, including the military, the DoS, USAID, the U.S. Information

Agency, and the CIA. Under CORDS, partnered civilian/military advisory teams were

dispatched throughout South Vietnam's 44 provinces and 250 districts.

The advisory teams brought holistic programs that were aimed at bringing a better

quality of life to the population focusing on the priorities of the specific districts. These

---

[20] William Westmoreland, "Westmoreland Military Advisory Command 0117 to BG James
Lawton Collins, Jr., Washington, 7 January 1966", *Westmoreland Files*, U.S. Army Center of Military
History (CMH), Fort McNair, Washington, D.C.,4.

[21] Dale Andrade and James H. Willbanks. "CORDS/Phoenix: Counterinsurgency Lessons from
Vietnam for the Future." *Military Review 86,* no 2. (March-April 2006): 11.

priorities ranged from land reform, medical care, schools, and agricultural assistance.[22]

"CORDS gave the pacification effort access to military money and personnel, allowing programs to expand dramatically. In 1966 there were about 1,000 advisers involved in pacification, and the annual budget was $582 million; by 1969 that had risen to 7,600 advisers and almost $1.5 billion."[23] The streamlined system under DoD control proved to be a catalyst that enabled and empowered other government agencies, assisting in rapid progress on the ground and civilian and military instruments of power integration.

CORDS placed military advisers and civilian interagency personnel under one civilian individual who was designated deputy MACV under General Westmoreland. With an equivalent 3-star and ambassadorial rank, Robert W. Komer orchestrated initial efforts with critical command of both interagency expertise and DoD resources. The marriage born of necessity against civilian agency wishes became a phenomenal success, just as unity of command in WWII occupation was two decades earlier. Unity of command succeeded where unity of effort had failed.[24]

Combined Action Platoons (CAP)

In Vietnam, U.S. Marines saw security of the population or pacification as the first tenant to a successful military strategy; second was the destruction of the enemy. Leading this approach in Vietnam was Marine Lieutenant General Charles Krulak, Commander of Fleet Marine Force- Pacific, and Lieutenant General Lewis Walt, Commander of the III Marine Amphibious Force. Securing the population was

---

[22] Andrade, 14.

[23] Dale Andrade, "Three Lessons from Vietnam," *Washington Post* (December 29, 2005).

[24] Lewis Sorley, A Better War: The Unexamined Victories and Final Tragedy of America's Last Years in Vietnam, (New York: Harcourt, Inc., 2000), 63.

paramount to success in Vietnam because it removed the ability of the enemy to operate

freely, denying the Vietcong (VC) and NVA the necessary infrastructure that supported

their missions.[25]

The goal of the CAP, was "to gain decisive results with the least application of

force and the consequent minimum loss of life. The end aim is the social, economic, and

political development of the people subsequent to the military defeat of the enemy

insurgent forces.[26] Persistent security, 24-hour presence, was the solution to the security

challenges in the villages.[27] "A soldier has to be much more than a man with a rifle

whose only objective is to kill. He has to be part diplomat, part technician, part

politician--and 100 percent a human being."[28]

The basic unit to execute this approach was a composite Marine squad of thirteen

Marines with additional enablers augmenting as required (forward observer, medic, Navy

corpsman) and partnered with a thirty five man South Vietnamese Popular Force (PF)

platoon. This partnered organization became known as a CAP.[29] The Marines, with the

assistance of the PF, provided permanent, round the clock defense to the villages—

persistent security. The difference was the permanent presence of the Marines which

provided the credibility and support the PF needed.

---

[25] Paul Melshen "The US Marines' Combined Action Program in Vietnam: The Formulation of Counterinsurgency Tactics within a Strategic Debate," *Low Intensity Conflict & Law Enforcement* Vol 9, no. 2 (Summer, 2000): 66.

[26] Lewis W. Walt, *Strange War, Strange Strategy: A General's Report on the War in Vietnam,* (New York: Funk and Wagnalls, 1970), 105.

[27] Bruce C. Almutt, Marine Combined Action Capabilities: The Vietnam Experience, Interim Technical Report, (McClean, VA: Human Sciences Research, Inc., 1969), 9.

[28] Terrence Maitland, *A Contagion of War (The Vietnam Experience),* (Boston: Boston Publishing Company, 2000), 23.

[29] Melshen, 72.

Equipped with an M1 and hand grenades, most PF were ineligible for service in the regular Army of the Republic of Vietnam and were considered the bottom of the force structure gene pool. Making less than ten dollars a month for pay, the PF received limited training, uniforms, or typical army gear. Prior to Marine partnership, most PF offered little resistance to the VC and often refused to defend the local population. General Walt, however, believed the PF soldier partnered with enabled Marines could be the turning point in the conflict. "He was defending his own home, family, and neighbors. He knew each paddy, field, trail, bush, or bamboo clump, each family shelter, tunnel, and buried rice urn."[30]

Leading by example, the Marines incrementally improved the capability of the PF. The Marines took the point on patrols, maneuvered after dark, fired aggressively on the enemy, and recorded the daily activity of all villagers creating a pattern of life revealing suspicious behavior. The partnership program worked extraordinarily well, and the PF responded with courage and creativity inspired by and emulating the Marine example. In fact, a CAP trained PF soldier was the first Vietnamese decorated by the United States with a Bronze Star for heroism.[31]

Formalization of the program resulted in six operational missions— destroy the enemy infrastructure within area of responsibility, provide security and rule of law, protect friendly infrastructure, secure lines of communications, organize an intelligence apparatus, and establish information operations against the VC.[32] The CAP would establish governance at the lowest level which would provide security, rule of law, and

---

[30] Walt, 88.

[31] Maitland, 63.

[32] Melshen, 72.

essential services to the population affording opportunities for a better life. "Unlike other combat forces in Vietnam, CAP platoons lived among the peasants and alongside their counterparts. Their cohabitation assured the villagers of their security. The resulting benefit derived from the relationship meant Marines were empowered with intelligence of their enemy that kept them alive."[33]

Despite quantifiable success, the CAP program received little support outside of Marine ranks and remained limited in scope. Unfortunately it contradicted the strategy that was being implemented by General Westmoreland; a search and destroy the enemy strategy that held little appreciation for the role of the populace. Marine Corps Commandant General Wallace M. Green would surmise, "From the very first, even before the first Marine battalion had landed in Da Nang, my feeling, a very strong one which I voiced to the Joint Chiefs, was that the real target in Vietnam was not the Vietcong and the North Vietnamese, but the Vietnamese people."[34] In his memoir of the Vietnam War, General Walt summed up what he believed to be the key to how to fight the war, "The struggle was in the rice paddies, in and among the people, not passing through, but living among them, night and day and joining with them in steps toward a better life long overdue."[35] CAP units provided persistent security to the population, enhancing their lifestyle with respect to rule of law and essential services, severed the

---

[33] Melshen,73.

[34] Jack Shulimson and Charles M. Johnson, *U.S. Marines in Vietnam: The Landing and the Buildup, 1965*, (Washington D.C.: Headquarters, U.S. Marine Corps, 1978), 46-47.

[35] Walt, 108.

enemy from their source of supply and recruitment, and defeated NVA and VC forces when in contact.[36]

Conclusion

The relevance of these lessons learned in current and future full spectrum operations across the continuum of conflict cannot be ignored. Several themes are consistent across the two historical case studies: the importance of unity of command, the importance of providing persistent security to the population and the civilian counterparts operating within the operational environment, the importance of educated soldiers prepared to quickly transition from high intensity combat to a governance mission or conduct both simultaneously. In each conflict, the military forces enabled civilian power to be employed. The military was the catalyst that allowed a whole-of-government approach to be executed. The next chapter will attempt to offer a menu of options that can be utilized to inform our national leadership about how the DoD can conduct the whole-of-government approach alone or with limited other government agency support.

---

[36] Melshen, 71.

CHAPTER 5:
CLOSING THE GAP

I am tempted indeed to declare dogmatically that whatever doctrine the Armed Forces are working on now, they have got it wrong. I am also tempted to declare that it does not matter that they have got it wrong. What does matter is their capacity to get it right quickly when the moment arrives.1

Sir Michael Howard

Sir Michael Howard is very astute in his observations about not only the U.S. military, but also our nation as a whole. Our government may misinterpret the strategic environment; adopt a myriad of ways counterintuitive to achieving our vital national interests, and argue and fight over the means required to achieve the whole-of-government approach; but what should not be lost, is that regardless of the direction our nation moves in, we must have the capacity and capability to get it right quickly when the moment arrives.

The intent of this chapter is to discuss a menu of options that could be developed or implemented to achieve our national interests utilizing the whole-of-government approach. The menu is informed by the earlier chapters and incrementally builds capability and capacity over time moving our government from a DoD only centric approach to a whole of nation strategy that meets the vision of our national leadership— a natural progression that is a product from learning from the past and understanding the future. The bottom line is that the DoD must be the catalyst for the whole-of-government approach to work.

---

[1] Michael Howard, "Military Science in the Age of Peace," Chesney Memorial Gold Medal Lecture, October 3, 1973, printed in *RUSI* [Royal United Services Institute] *Journal* (March 1974).

DoD Alone

General Peter Chiarelli, the Vice Chairman of U. S. Army, in a speech to the Marine Corps University on January 3, 2008, clearly expressed the dissatisfaction of the DoD, "while the US government has begun to take steps to increase state department funding and capabilities, it is more likely that, the interagency will be broken for our lifetime."[2] The DoD cannot rely on a broken interagency when our national interests are in jeopardy, failure is not an option.

Several possible opportunities are available to ensure that the DoD can execute the whole-of-government mission alone. First, a military whole-of-government center of excellence could be established, followed by the creation of a standalone whole-of-government unit that could implement doctrine and procedures developed by the center of excellence. Third, the roles of our citizen soldiers could be expanded and institutionalized taking advantage of their unique citizen-soldier qualities and, finally, a school for military government could be established to create the military whole-of-government professional.

Military Whole-of-Government Center of Excellence

Our nation was confronted with a very similar irony following Vietnam, what steps could be taken to ensure that our military was prepared for the next conflict. One of the recommendations is uniquely relevant today, as retired Marine Colonel Paul Melshen suggests:

> during periods of peacetime or periods of engagement in conventional warfare, militaries seldom value the need for a unit established for the sole purpose of the research and study of counterinsurgency warfare. Nothing could be greater folly.

---

[2] Peter Chiarelli, Speech to the Marine Corps University, (January 2008).

A military organization must establish a small unit or organization which is dedicated to the purpose of the research, study development, and employment of effective counterinsurgency tactics, operations, and strategy.[3]

By replacing counterinsurgency warfare with the whole-of-government strategy, significant parallels become apparent. A whole-of-government center of excellence should be a conduit for all lessons learned, studying the approach throughout history across the entire spectrum of conflict; what worked and why did it work. The center of excellence would be the start point for commanders, civilian leaders, and staffs to draw upon analysis.

Stand Alone Whole-of-Government Unit of Action

In recent years, many observers have concluded that the DoD excels at winning wars, but has failed to develop equivalent interagency capabilities to win the peace.[4] The next logical progression for this center of excellence would be to actually provide the capability into the fight. "Retired General Anthony Zinni argued in September 2009 that simply increasing the budgets and personnel of the civilian agencies would compound the problem, and proposed instead the creation of a military command that would organize, structure, and deploy in support of humanitarian and reconstruction efforts."[5] The DoD should not only focus on its strengths, security related tasks such as providing civil security and control, but should also develop a specialized unit to institutionalize DoD capabilities to train foreign military police and border guards.[6]

---

[3] Melshen, "Mapping Out a Counterinsurgency Strategy," 682.

[4] Brent Scowcroft and Samuel R. Berger, "In the Wake of War: Getting Serious about Nation-Building," *The National Interest*, no. 81 (Fall 2005): 49.

[5] Nikolas Gvosdev and Derek S. Reveron, "Waging War, Building States," *Policy Review,* no. 163 (October 2010): 7.

[6] David W. Shin, "U.S. Army, Narrowing the Gap: DoD and Stability Operations," *Military Review* (April 2009): 54.

Expand the National Guard and Reserve Forces

Many of the complex missions facing our military in Iraq and Afghanistan are not resident within the active DoD and require specialized skills. The strongest argument in favor of maintaining a strong operational reserve component is the opportunity for the U.S. military to draw upon cutting-edge skills and knowledge from the civilian world. Reserve component service members have civilian backgrounds and careers that provide them with unique expertise, particularly in specialized and high-tech fields, which is generally difficult to locate, train, and retain in the active component.[7]

The different instruments of national power exists within the DoD, and unfortunately have not been fully utilized. Our citizen soldiers, National Guard and Reserve forces, provide the DoD with a distinct combination of military and civilian skills. The dual nature of citizen soldiers allows them to be effective when conducting military and civilian power missions simultaneously. The National Guard has been conducting civil-military missions in Central America, Eastern Europe, South and Central America for two decades and is heavily involved in operations in Afghanistan.

The State Partnership Program, Agri-Business Development Teams, and Training and Reconstruction Teams are excellent examples of the National Guard using a combination of civilian and military power expertise to support the geographical combatant commanders' theater campaign plans.[8] The State Partnership Program links U.S. states with partner country's active and reserve forces. Currently the program is

---

[7] Gregory F. Treverton, David Oaks, Lynn M. Scott, Justin L. Adams and Stephen Dalzell, *Attracting "CuttingEdge" Skills Through Reserve Component Participation,* (Santa Monica, CA: RAND, 2003), 17.

[8] Craig McKinley, *The National Guard a Great Value for America,* (Washington D.C.: National Guard Bureau, July 2010), 7.

partnered with 63 foreign countries supporting the engagement strategy of the combatant commander. Agri-Business Development Teams from twelve farm-belt states have deployed to Afghanistan facilitating sustainable projects that aid the Afghan people in a manner that results in greater impact and more long term benefits. Since 2002, Provincial Training and Reconstruction Teams (PRTs) in Iraq and Afghanistan have been provided security with augmentation from a National Guard platoon or company.

DoD should standardize National Guard and Reserve Component unit structures ensuring that these types of requirements remain manned, trained, and properly equipped. As General James Jones, European Command Combatant Commander, said in 2006, "The unique expertise the Guard and Reserve units bring to Civil Affairs, Information and Psychological Operations, and many other aspects of our high demand, low-density type capabilities that are in such precious supply, are absolutely critical to the execution of our future strategy."[9] One cannot argue that in a strategic environment where operations occur across the full spectrum of conflict, that "individuals possessing a wider repertoire of military and nonmilitary abilities will prove invaluable during complex operations involving military, political, economic and technological lines of effort."[10]

School of Military Governance

General MacArthur's success in post-war Japan can be directly linked to the foresight establishing the School of Military Government in 1942. The importance of educated military soldiers schooled in governance was not lost on him, and he would later comment to that effect:

---

[9] *Commission on the National Guard and Reserves*, http://www.cngr.gov/ (accessed February 11, 2011).

[10] Thomas X. Hammes, *The Sling and the Stone*, (Minneapolis: Zenith Press, 2006), 273.

Skilled officers, like all other professional men, are products of continuous and laborious study, training, and experience. There is no shortcut to the peculiar type of knowledge and ability they must possess. Trained officers constitute the most vitally essential element in modern war, and the only one that under no circumstance can be improvised or extemporized.[11]

DoD Instruction 3000.05 says stability operations tasks include rebuilding host nation institutions— security forces, correctional facilities, and judicial systems; reviving the private sector by promoting economic activity and infrastructure development; and developing representative government institutions.[12] The military is also directed to conduct these tasks in absence of civilian power, if none of these tasks are resident within the military, than the conclusion is simple, learn from the past and implement a military education system to train the force to meet the requirements of the whole-of-government approach.

Combined Interagency Initiatives

"War and diplomacy are different but intimately related aspects of national policy. Diplomats and warriors who recall this will therefore act as brothers in a potentially lethal common endeavor. They will consider together when to fight and when to talk and when to press and when to stop."[13] The DoD conducting the whole-of-government approach alone is not the ideal solution; clearly the experts of civilian power can offer more, with respect to non-military requirements, than this author, an artilleryman, can. As all our national security professionals are quick to offer, a blending and balance of the

---

[11] Edward T. Imparato, *General MacArthur Speeches and Reports 1908-1964,* (Atlanta, GA: Turner Publishing Company, 2000), 42.

[12] United States Department of Defense, Interim Progress Report on DoD Directive 3000.05; Military Support for Stability, Security, Transition, and Reconstruction (SSTR) Operations, Office of the Under Secretary of Defense for Policy, (August 2006), 6.

[13] Chas. W. Freeman, Jr., *The Diplomat's Dictionary*, (National Defense University Press, 1995), 33.

instruments of power is required to optimize the effectiveness of the whole-of-government approach.

Establish an Interagency Command

"If we are to meet the myriad challenges around the world in the coming decades, this country must strengthen other important elements of national power, both institutionally and financially, and create the capability to integrate and apply all of the elements of national power to problems and challenges abroad."[14] Despite Secretary Gates urging, the lack of capacity in other U.S. departments and agencies remains the primary challenge in integrating DoD activities with interagency partners. Changing this fundamental dynamic will require persuading a resistant Congress to dedicate additional resources to other agencies for participation in operations across the full spectrum of conflict, alongside of, or instead of, U.S. military forces.

Over the past several years, U.S. Government agencies have been revising their thinking on counterinsurgency and stability operations. Despite recent doctrine and guidance about better ways to end conflict and promote lasting peace, however, something has been missing from the dialogue— a successful model.[15] A successful model does exist, yet is overlooked as the natural progression for interagency cooperation and collaboration; the Joint Forces Command (JFCOM). Utilizing the JFCOM model, an interagency command should be established.

Following the passage of the Goldwater-Nichols Act in 1986, military leaders, key government officials and congressmen expressed a desire for a better process to

---

[14] National Defense Strategy, 12.

[15] William A. Stuebner and Richard Hirsch, "Mindanao: A Community-based Approach to Counterinsurgency," *Prism*, no. 3, vol. 1(June 2010): 129.

improve interoperability among the services. Consequently, on October 1, 1999, JFCOM

was established to do just that. The JFCOM mission is to provide mission-ready, joint

capable forces and support the development and integration of joint, interagency, and

multinational capabilities to meet the present and future operational needs of the joint

force.[16] The mission has three distinct elements— providing joint capable forces,

developing and integrating joint capabilities, and determining future requirements to

support the force.

Vice Chairman of Joint Chiefs of Staff, General James Cartwright, in testimony in

front of the House Armed Services Committee offered in 2010:

> When JFCOM was stood up in 1999, its central mission was to drive jointness
> into everything the military does. It was understood that the creation of JFCOM
> for this purpose would result in the addition of an organization layer. At that
> time, it was judged that the imperative to advance jointness was greater than the
> costs associated with establishing a new command. Jointness is difficult to
> measure, but the goal of embracing joint operations and doctrine has reached a
> point where a four-star headquarters for joint advocacy is no longer required. We
> have embraced jointness as a matter of necessity. Evidence of this progression is
> manifested on the battlefield and in our military schools. We have reached
> critical mass, where our military accepts "joint" as the preferred method of war.[17]

If you substitute *joint* with *whole-of-government* and use the same logic postulated by

General Cartwright, then you come to a very simple conclusion, the imperative to

advance the whole-of-government approach outweighs any cost associated with

establishing a new command. "Success in attaining jointness has been manifested in the

execution of joint warfare— America now fights wars almost solely under joint

commands. There have been pronounced successes toward jointness made in

---

[16] United States Joint Forces Command, "Command Overview Briefing," (Norfolk, VA: Office of
Public Affairs, U.S. Joint Forces Command, August 6, 2010), slide 2.

[17] Statement of General James E. Cartwright, USMC Vice Chairman of the Joint Chiefs of Staff,
before the House Armed Services Committee (Wednesday, September 29th, 2010).

peacetime— the evolution in joint doctrine and exercises."[18] JFCOM, a command born out of necessity to improve the interoperability among the services, is a model that should be emulated to create an interagency command to improve the whole-of-government approach.

Interagency Training Center

As mentioned earlier, the INSPEAD Act is a great beginning to creating leaders that have the qualities of flexibility, agility, adaptability, and the ability to build unique teams of teams to accomplish missions utilizing the whole-of-government approach.[19] The surge in Afghanistan and the transition from military power to civilian power in Iraq has led to another great initiative that must be expanded and institutionalized, the Civilian Training Center at Camp Atterbury, Indiana.[20]

The civilians trained at Camp Atterbury take a crash course learning rules of engagement, cultural and language differences, and basic risks within the operational environment. "More than 70,000 personnel have been trained for deployment here since 2003. Experience gained in conducting these trial courses eventually could lead to Camp Atterbury developing into a national deployment center for civilians in addition to its current role as a military mobilization hub."[21] The center provides a neutral environment for the civilians where they are not immediately thrust within a military environment.

---

[18] Don M. Snider, "Jointness, Defense Transformation, and the Need for a New Joint Warfare Profession," *Parameters* (Autumn, 2003): 17.

[19] National Military Strategy, 16.

[20] John Crosby, "Civilian Surge Comes to Life at Camp Atterbury," (Camp Atterbury, IN: *Indiana National Guard Press* (December 3, 2010), 1.

[21] Ibid., 2.

The military assimilation is as critical a task as cultural awareness is for the country the civilians will deploy to.

DoD as the Catalyst

The DoD could transform into two very distinct forces, the force that wins the war and the force that wages the peace.

> The U.S. military's war fighting capacity and the high performance combat troops, weapon systems, aircraft, armor, and ships associated with all-out war against traditionally defined opponents. This is the force America created to defend the West against the Soviet threat, now transformed from its industrial-era roots to its information-age capacity for high-speed, high-lethality, and high-precision major combat operations.[22]

The U.S. military is without peer in the world today, creating an environment where our current and future enemies will seek to avoid direct confrontation and instead attempt to wage an asymmetrical war focusing on economic interests and civilian resolve or will. The force designed to win the war is not created for the transition to peace operations which include post conflict stabilization, reconstruction operations, and counterinsurgency campaigns.[23]

The second force, a non-lethal variant designed to wage the peace, "is optimized for stability and support operations, post conflict stabilization, reconstruction operations, humanitarian assistance/disaster relief, and any and all operations associated with low-intensity conflict, counterinsurgency operations, and small-scale crisis response."[24] The force is populated with a police component capable of providing civil security and civilian personnel with expertise in not only security, but essential services, rule of law,

---

[22] Barnett, 430.

[23] Ibid., 431.

[24] Ibid., 432

66

and governance able to rebuilding networks, infrastructure, and social and political institutions. "While the core security and logistical capabilities are derived from uniformed military components, this force is fundamentally envisioned as a standing capacity for interagency and international collaboration in nation-building."[25]

Conclusion

The National Security System is slowly evolving; however, the system remains founded in the Cold War era, compartmentalized and un-collaborative. Change must be substantial and occur more rapidly if our nation is to achieve our national security objectives utilizing the whole-of-government approach as directed by our President.

> Integrating the civilian agencies of our government into these efforts will require structural and cultural changes in the executive and legislative branches, a comprehensive strategic planning process for national security, integrating all elements of national power, and provides the requisite guidance to the relevant federal departments and agencies that must work together to confront this century's challenges.[26]

"As we think about enhancing our whole-of-nation efforts, important questions remain. What are the fundamentals in a campaign? How do we educate and train ourselves to build the capacity for a broad-based national effort? How do we work together before we are in a conflict? How do we plan together?"[27]

To answer these questions, our leaders can provide more unattainable rhetoric, or because the whole-of-government approach is imperative to advancing or achieving our

---

[25] Barnett, 432

[26] Stephen J. Hadley and William J. Perry, "What Needs to Change to Defend America," *Washington Post* (August 1, 2010): 6.

[27] Mike Mullen, "Working Together: Modern Challenges Need "Whole-of-Nation" Effort," *Joint Forces Quarterly* (October 2010): 32.

vital national interests, the cost to establishing and implementing holistic DOTMLPF

initiatives is nonnegotiable. Failure is not an option.

CONCLUSION

Drawing from experiences during the Malayan Emergency, British General Sir Frank Kitson warns, "The first thing that must be apparent when contemplating the sort of action which a government facing insurgency should take, is that there can be no such thing as a purely military solution because insurgency is not primarily a military activity."[1] In the most recent NSS, President Obama, understanding that military power should be implemented and balanced with civilian power, directs for a whole-of-government approach to be adopted in achieving our vital national interests.[2] Secretary of State Clinton echoes the President in her QDDR. However, the DoD acknowledges that despite considerable urging and support, the lack of capacity in other U.S. departments and agencies remains the primary challenge in integrating DoD activities with interagency partners.[3]

Changing this fundamental dynamic will require persuading a resistant Congress to dedicate additional resources to other U.S. agencies for participation in full spectrum operations alongside or instead of U.S. military forces. In a large-scale effort, not unlike WWII or the Vietnam War, a shortage of personnel from non-DoD agencies will require the use of DoD personnel, including civilians, reservists, and retirees, who possess critical non-military skills in governance, rule of law, and development. Lessons from historical examples can also prepare the DoD to properly execute missions along the

---

[1] Frank Kitson, *Bunch of Five,* (London: Faber and Faber, 1977), 283.

[2] National Security Strategy, 17.

[3] DoD Directive 3000.05, 2.

69

operational continuum and across the full spectrum of conflict alone or with limited support.

Over the next quarter century, U.S. military forces will be continually engaged in some dynamic combination of combat, security, engagement, and relief and reconstruction. "In this environment, the presence, reach, and capability of U.S. military forces, working with like-minded partners, will continue to be called upon to protect our national interests."[4] How can the U.S. perform these missions in the future and prevent a continuation of poor performance as seen in Iraq and Afghanistan today?

First, the U.S. government must realize that the civilian instruments of power have limited capability and capacity to contribute across the spectrum of conflict and throughout the entire continuum of operations. Understanding the requirement for a whole-of-government approach and likewise addressing it in a strategy document does not equal the ability to implement. Second, with this realism, adequately resource and prepare the DoD to execute the whole-of-government approach independently, with little or no assistance, and, finally, incrementally build civilian power capacity and capability relieving the DoD from non-military responsibilities.

A strategy to implement the strategy must be developed; in the meantime, the DoD must be prepared to conduct a whole-of-government approach alone or with limited support from the other government agencies and departments. As Admiral Mike Mullen concludes, "Just because a soldier can do it, that doesn't mean a soldier should do it. But I'm fearful that, by default, and in spite of strong efforts by the State Department and its

---

[4] United States Joint Forces Command, *The Joint Operating Environment*, (Norfolk, VA, 2010), 4.

leadership, many missions that should be done by civilians may still fall on your broad shoulders."[5]

_____

[5] Kevin Baron, "White House Struggling to Budge Congess on Civilian Aid for Wars," *Stars and Stripes* (December 6, 2010).

BIBLIOGRAPHY

Andrade, Dale. "Three Lessons from Vietnam." *Washington Post* (December 29, 2005).

--., and James H. Willbanks. "CORDS/Phoenix: Counterinsurgency Lessons from Vietnam for the Future." *Military Review 86,* no. 2 (March-April 2006): 9-23.

"Assistant Secretary of Defense for Special Operations/Low-Intensity Conflict & Interdependent Capabilities." Office of the Under Secretary of Defense for Policy. http://policy.defense.gov/solic/psso/usgcapabilities.aspx (accessed March 8, 2011).

Allnutt, Bruce C. *Marine Combined Action Capabilities: The Vietnam Experience; Interim Technical Report.* McLean, Va.: Human Sciences Research, 1969.

Andrews, Tom. "Classified McChrystal Report: 500,000 Troops Will Be Required Over Five Years in Afghanistan." *Huffingtonpost* , September 12, 2009.

Bankus, Brent C., and James Kievit. "The Army and Marines and Military Government." *Small Wars Journal* online, http://smallwarsjournal.com/documents/bankuskievit.doc (accessed 28 February 2011).

Barnett, Thomas P. M. *Great Powers: America and the World After Bush.* New York: G.P. Putnam's Sons, 2009.

Baron, Kevin. "White House Struggling to Budget Congress on Civilian Aid for Wars." *Stars and Stripes*, December 6, 2010.

Berntsen, Gary, and Ralph Pezzullo. *Jawbreaker: The Attack on Bin Laden and Al Qaeda : A Personal Account by the CIA's Key Field Commander.* New York: Crown Publishers, 2005.

Binnendijk, Hans, and Stuart E. Johnson. *Transforming for Stabilization and Reconstruction Operations.* Ft. Belvoir: Defense Technical Information Center, 2004.

Blakeman, Kathryn, and William B. Skelton. *2008-2009 Annual Edition: Journal for the Study of Peace and Conflict.* Madison, WI: Wisconsin Institute for Peace and Conflict Studies, 2008.

Bloom, Harold. *George Bernard Shaw's Man and Superman.* New York: Chelsea House, 1987.

Brooks, D.A., and P.J. Candreva. "Whither the Defense Budget?" *Journal of Financial Management* (Spring, 2008): 13-18.

Caldwell IV, William B., and Steven M. Leonard. "Field Manual 3-07, Stability Operations: Upshifting the Engine of Change." *Military Review* 88, no. 4 (July-August, 2008): 6-13.

Cambone, Stephen A. *A New Structure for National Security Policy Planning.* Washington, D.C.: Center for Strategic and International Studies, 1998.

Carafano, James J. "Budgets and Threats: An Analysis of Strategic Priorities for Maritime Security." *The Heritage Foundation* no. 791 (June 16, 2003): 1-12.

--. *Post-Conflict Operations from Europe to Iraq.* Washington, D.C.: Heritage Foundation, 2004.

Cartwright, James E. House Armed Services Committee statement, September 29, 2010.

Clausewitz, Carl von. *On War.* New York: Knopf, 1993.

Clinton, Hillary R. "Leading Through Civilian Power." *Foreign Affairs,* (November/December 2010): 10-14.

--. "Promoting Security through Diplomacy and Development: The Fiscal Year 2011 International Affairs Budget." Secretary of State Opening Remarks before the House Foreign Affairs Committee. February 25, 2010. Washington, D.C.

Coats, Jason, and Mike Ryan. "The U.S.-Iraq Security Agreement." *Military Review* (September/October 2009): 48-53.

Coffey, Ross. "Revisiting CORDS: The Need for Unity of Effort to Secure Victory in Iraq." *Military Review* 86, no. 2 (March/April 2006): 24-34.

Chiarelli, Peter. Speech to the Marine Corps University (January 2008).

--. "Training Full Spectrum: Less Is More." *Army Magazine* (June 2009): 11.

Christensen, Tom, and Per Laegreid. "The Whole-of-Government Approach to Public Sector Reform." Public Administration Review no 67 (November/December 2007): 1059-1066.

Colas, Harry Lewis, and Albert Katz Weinberg. *Civil Affairs: Soldiers Become Governors.* Washington, D.C.: Center of Military History, 2004.

Coll, Steve. *Ghost Wars: The Secret History of the CIA, Afghanistan, and bin Laden, from the Soviet Invasion to September 10, 2001.* New York: Penguin Press, 2004.

Commission on the National Guard and Reserves. http://www.cngr.gov/ (accessed

February 11, 2011).

Corum, James S. *Training Indigenous Forces in Counterinsurgency a Tale of Two Insurgencies*. Carlisle, PA: Strategic Studies Institute, U.S. Army War College, 2006.

Crane, Conrad C., and W. Andrew Terrill. "Reconstructing Iraq: Insights, Challenges, and Missions for Military Forces in a Post-Conflict Scenario." Monograph. Strategic Studies Institute, U.S. Army War College, February 2003.

Crosby, John. "Civilian Surge Comes to Life at Camp Atterbury." *Indiana National Guard Press*, December 3, 2010.

Davis, Geoff. "Legislation Targeted at Reforming National Security." *AUSA News*, February 1, 2011.

Dempsey, Martin. "Versatility as Institutional Imperative." *Small Wars Journal* (May 4, 2009).

Dobbins, James. *The Beginner's Guide to Nation-Building*. Santa Monica, CA: Rand National Security Research Division, 2007.

Evans, Judith. *The Project on National Security Reform Releases Recommendations Urging Sweeping Changes to Improve the U.S. National Security System*. Washington D.C.: Project for National Security Reform, 2008.

Flournoy, Michele. "USG Civilian Capabilities." Office for the Undersecretary of Defense for Policy. http://policy.defense.gov/solic/psso/usgcapabilities.aspx (accessed February 28, 2011).

Fontenot, Gregory, E. J. Degen, and David Tohn. *On Point: The United States Army in Operation Iraqi Freedom*. Official U.S. Government ed. Fort Leavenworth, Kansas: Combat Studies Institute Press: 2004.

Forging a New Shield. Arlington,VA: Center for the Study of the Presidency, Project on National Security Reform, 2008.

Freeman, Charles W. *The Diplomat's Dictionary*. Washington, DC: National Defense University Press, 1994.

Garomone, Jim. "Balance at Heart of New Defense Strategy." *Small Wars Journal* (July 31, 2008): 22-24.

Gates, Robert M. "A Balanced Strategy: Reprogramming the Pentagon for a New Age." *DISAM Journal of International Security Assistance Management*, no. 31 (March 2009): 12.

Global Trends 2025 A Transformed World. Washington, D.C.: National Intelligence

Council, 2008.

Gockel, Kathy. "Meeting Complex Challenges Through National Security Reforms."
    INSS Proceedings, (October 2008): 6-8.

Gvosdev, Nikolas, and Derek S. Reveron. "Waging War, Building States." *Policy
    Review*, no. 163 (October 2010): 44-51.

Gray, Colin S. *Defense Planning, Surprise and Prediction*. Brussels, Belgium: 80.

Griffith, Samuel B., and B.H. Liddell Hart. *The Art of War*. London: Oxford University
    Press, 1971.

Gurney, D.H. "Executive Summary." *Joint Forces Quarterly*, no. 57 (2nd Quarter 2010):
    7.

Hadley, Stephen J., and William J. Perry. "What Needs to Change to Defend America."
Washington Post, August 1, 2010.

Hammes, Thomas X. *The Sling and the Stone: On War in the 21st Century*. St. Paul, MN:
    Zenith Press, 2004.

Hoff, Ebbe Curtis, John Lada, and Richard R. Taylor. *Civil Affairs/Military Government
    Public Health Activities*. Washington, D.C.: Office of the Surgeon General, Dept.
    of the Army, 1976.

Howard, Michael. "Military Science in the Age of Peace." *RUSI Journal* (March 1974).

Imparato, Edward T. *General MacArthur: Speeches and Reports 1908-1964*. Paducah,
    KY: Turner Pub., 2000.

Jennings, Ray Salvatore. *The Road Ahead: Lessons in Nation Building from Japan,
    Germany, and Afghanistan for Postwar Iraq*. Washington, DC: U.S. Institute of
    Peace, 2003.

Kem, Jack. "INSPEAD: Going Beyond Goldwater-Nichols." Fort Leavenworth, Kansas:
    Combined Arms Center, October 2, 2010.

Kitson, Frank. *Bunch of Five*. London: Faber, 1977.

Kohl, Jen. "Proposed Bill Seeks to Improve Security Collaboration - CNN." Featured
    Articles from *CNN*. http://articles.cnn.com/2010-09-
    30/politics/house.security.bill_1_skelton-national-security-
    collaboration?_s=PM:POLITICS (accessed March 8, 2011).

Komer, R. W. *The Malayan Emergency in Retrospect: Organization of a Successful
    Counterinsurgency Effort*. Santa Monica, CA.: RAND, 1972.

Lada, John. *Civil Affairs/Military Government Public Health Activities, Preventive Medicine in World War II.* Washington D.C.: Office of the Surgeon General United States Army, 1976.

Lapping, Brian. *End of Empire.* New York: St. Martin's Press, 1985.

Lew, Jacob L. "President's Proposal for the FY 2011 State Department Budget." Washington D.C.: Deputy Secretary for Management and Resources (February 1, 2010).

Maitland, Terrence. *The Vietnam Experience: A Contagion of War.* Boston, MA: Boston Publishing Company, 1983.

Mancuso, Mario. "Irregular Warfare Roadmap." *Special Operations Technology*, vol. 9, iss. 1 (February 2011): 19-23.

McKinley, Craig R. *The National Guard a Great Value for America.* Arlington, VA, 2010.

Melshen, Paul. "Mapping Out a Counterinsurgency Campaign Plan: Critical Considerations in Counterinsurgency Campaigning." *Small Wars and Insurgencies*, 18, no. 4 (December 2007): 665-698.

--. "The U.S. Marines' Combined Action Program in Vietnam: The Formulation of Counterinsurgency Tactics within a Strategic Debate." *Low Intensity Conflict & Law Enforcement* vol. 9, no. 2 (Summer, 2000).

Mitchell, Andrea. "Fortress America, New U.S. Embassy in Iraq Cloaked in Mystery." *New York Times*, April 14, 2006.

Mullen, Mike. "Working Together: Modern Challenges Need "Whole of Nation" Effort." *Joint Forces Quarterly* no. 59 (October 2010): 2.

National Security Act of 1947: P.L. 80-253. Ithaca, N.Y.: Cornell Law Library, 1947.

Nestler, Scott T. "TTHS is Not a Four-Letter Word." *Institute for Land Warfare* Essay no. 04-7W. Association of the United States Army: November 2004.

Obama, Barak . "The Way Forward in Afghanistan and Pakistan." Address to the Nation from United States Military Academy, West Point, NY, December 1, 2009.

"Office of the Coordinator for Reconstruction and Stabilization (S/CRS): Civilian Response Corps." Office of the Coordinator for Reconstruction and Stabilization (S/CRS): Home Page. http://www.crs.state.gov/index.cfm?fuseaction=public.display&shortcut=4QRB

(accessed March 8, 2011).

Percy, Jason L., and Terry A. Fellows Jr. "A Whole of Government Approach for National Strategy." Master's Thesis, Monterey, CA: Naval Postgraduate School, 2009.

Rogin, Josh. "Ros-Lehtinen, My Mission is to Cut the State and Foreign Aid Budgets." *The Cable*, December 8, 2010.

Scowcroft, Brent, and Samuel Berger. "In the Wake of War: Getting Serious About Nation-Building." *The National Interest* . (September 2005): 49-52.

Shaw, George Bernard. *Man and Superman.* Cambridge, MA: The University Press, 1903.

Shin, David W. "U.S. Army, Narrowing the Gap: DoD and Stability Operations." *Military Review* (April 2009): 53-54.

Shinseki, Eric. Senate Armed Services Committee testimony (February 25, 2003).

Shulimson, Jack, and Charles M. Johnson. *U.S. Marines in Vietnam: The Landing and the Buildup 1965.* Washington D.C.: History and Museums Division Headquarters, U.S. Marine Corps, 1978.

Snider, Don M. "Jointness, Defense Transformation, and the Need for a New Joint Warfare Profession." *Parameters* (Autumn, 2003): 17-18.

Sorley, Lewis. *A Better War: The Unexamined Victories and Final Tragedy of America's Last Years in Vietnam.* New York: Harcourt Brace & Co., 1999.

Stuebner, William A., and Richard Hirsch. "Mindanao: A Community-based Approach to Counterinsurgency." *Prism*, vol. 1, no. 3 (June 2010):127-131.

The National Military Strategy of the United States of America. Washington D.C.: White House, 2011.

The National Security Strategy of the United States of America. Washington D.C.: White House, 2011.

Treverton, Gregory F., David Oaks, Lynn M. Scott, Justin L. Adams and Stephen Dalzell. *Attracting "CuttingEdge" Skills Through Reserve Component Participation.* Santa Monica, CA: RAND, 2003.

United States Department of the Army. *Leadership Statements and Quotes: Department of the Army Pamphlet 600-65.* Washington D.C.: U.S. Government Printing Office, 1985.

--. *Operations: FM 3-0*. Washington D.C.: U.S. Government Printing Office, 2008.

--. *Tactics, Techniques and Procedures for Fire Support for the Combined Arms Commander: FM 3-09.31*. Washington D.C.: U.S. Government Printing Office, 2002.

--. *Training For Full Spectrum Operations: FM 7-0*. Washington D.C.: U.S. Government Printing Office, 2008.

United States Department of Defense. "Civilian Expeditionary Work Force." Civilian Personnel Management Service. http://www.cpms.osd.mil/expeditionary/cew-secretary-message.aspx (accessed March 8, 2011).

--. *Department of Defense Instruction Number 1120.11:Programming and Accounting for Active Military Manpower*. [Washington D.C.]: Joint Chiefs of Staff, 2007.

--. *Department of Defense Instruction Number 3000.05: Stability Operations*. [Washington D.C.]: Joint Chiefs of Staff, 2009.

--. *Directive 3000.05, Military Support for Security, Stability, Transition and Reconstruction (SSTR)*. [Washington D.C.]: Joint Chiefs of Staff, 2005.

--. *Doctrine for the Armed Forces of the United States: JP 1-0*. [Washington D.C.]: Joint Chiefs of Staff, 2009.

--. *Interim Progress Report on DoD Directive 3000.05; Military Support for Stability, Security, Transition, and Reconstruction (SSTR) Operations*. [Washington D.C.]: Office for the Undersecretary of Defense for Policy, 2006.

--. *Irregular Warfare: Countering Irregular Threats: Joint Operating Concept, Version 2.0* [Washington D.C.]: Joint Chiefs of Staff, 2010.

--. *Joint Operations: JP 3-0 Change 2*. [Washington D.C.]: Joint Chiefs of Staff, 2010.

--. *Quadrennial Defense Review Report*. [Washington D.C.]: Joint Chiefs of Staff, 2010.

--. *Report to Congress on the Implementation Progress of DoD 3000.05*. [Washington D.C.]: Office for the Undersecretary of Defense for Policy, 2007.

United States Department of State. "Civil Response Corps." Office for Reconstruction and Stabilization. http://www.crs.state.gov/index.cfm?fuseaction=public.display&shortcut=4QRB (accessed February 28, 2011).

--. "President Issues Directive to Improve the United States' Capacity to Manage

Reconstruction and Stabilization Efforts."
http://www.fas.org/irp/offdocs/nspd/nspd-44fs.html (accessed April 25, 2011).

--. *The First Quadrennial Diplomacy and Development Review*. [Washington D.C.]:
Secretary of State, 2010.

United States Joint Forces Command. "Command Overview Briefing." Norfolk, VA:
Office of Public Affairs, August 6, 2010, slide 2.

--. *The JOE, Joint Operating Environment, 2010*. Norfolk, VA.

United States President Directive. "National Security Presidential Directive/NSPD-44."
Washington: White House, 2005.

Walt, Lewis W. *Strange War, Strange Strategy; A General's Report on Vietnam*. New
York: Funk & Wagnalls, 1970.

Warner, Rex. *Thucydides: History of the Peloponnesian War*. Harmondsworth,
Middlesex: Penguin, 1954.

Weinberger, Caspar W. *Fighting for Peace: Seven Critical Years in the Pentagon*. New
York, NY: Warner Books, 1990.

Westmoreland, William C. "Westmoreland Military Advisory Command 0117 to BG James
Lawton Collins, Jr., Washington, 7 January 1966." *Westmoreland Files*. Fort McNair, Washington, D.C.:
U.S. Army Center of Military History.

Yarger, Harry R. *Strategy and the National Security Professional: Strategic Thinking and
Strategy Formulation in the 21st Century*. Westport, CT.: Praeger Security
International, 2008.

Ziemke, Earl Frederick. *The U.S. Army in the Occupation of Germany, 1944-1946*.
Washington, D.C.: Center of Military History, United States Army, 1975.

www.ingramcontent.com/pod-product-compliance
Lightning Source LLC
Chambersburg PA
CBHW081847280526
45789CB00007B/2598